CW00400762

MAKE YOUR HOME A NATURE RESERVE

First published 2024 by The O'Brien Press Ltd.,
12 Terenure Road East, Rathgar, Dublin 6, D06 HD27, Ireland.
Tel: +353 1 4923333; Fax: +353 1 4922777
E-mail: books@obrien.ie. Website: obrien.ie
The O'Brien Press is a member of Publishing Ireland.

ISBN: 978-1-78849-472-4

Copyright for text © Donna Mullen 2024
The moral rights of the author have been asserted
Copyright for typesetting, layout, design © The O'Brien Press Ltd.
Cover design by Anne O'Hara
Internal design by Emma Byrne
Animal illustrations by Eoin O'Brien
Sonogram illustrations by Fionn Keeley
Author photograph by Brian Keeley

All rights reserved. No part of this publication may be reproduced or utilised in
any form or by any means, electronic or mechanical, including for text and data
mining, training artificial intelligence systems, photocopying, recording or in any
information storage and retrieval system, without permission in writing from the
publisher.

10 9 8 7 6 5 4 3 2 1
28 27 26 25 24

Printed in the UK by Clays Ltd, St Ives plc.
The paper in this book is produced using pulp from managed forests.

Published in

MAKE YOUR HOME A NATURE RESERVE

Donna Mullen

THE O'BRIEN PRESS
DUBLIN

DONNA MULLEN has worked as an ecologist for over thirty years and is a founding member of Bat Conservation Ireland and the Irish Environmental Network. She met her husband at a bat group meeting, and together they bought a farm in Meath and turned it into Golashane Nature Reserve. The reserve, home to several people and hundreds of plants, birds, mammals, insects and amphibians, has won several awards, including an EU Rural Inspiration award. Every week someone arrives at the door to ask how to create a nature reserve in their own home.

DEDICATION

Every little creature matters, from the tiny wood
mouse to the spectacular barn owl. And what you
do matters too. So, if you are helping wildlife in
any way, open a bottle of wine or munch into a
cream cake. Because what you are doing is vitally
important. You are wonderful, and this book is
dedicated to you. Take a bow!

CONTENTS

INTRODUCTION

When I was a kid, I wanted to own a nature reserve. Preferably in a hot place, perhaps somewhere in Africa, where gazelle and giraffe would casually walk by. It took years before it dawned on me that in fact, I did own several nature reserves. They took the forms of window boxes, back gardens and finally a farm in north Meath. There is more wind and rain than in my African dream, but the animals around me are just as interesting when you get to know them. And they may even be under more threat here, where we intensively use the land for our food, fuel and homes.

Most wildlife books give you facts and figures on the size, weight and shape of an animal. But that doesn't interest me. I am 170cm, 65kg and have an upper arm length of 38cm. But what does that tell you about me? Unless you wish to buy me a dress, that information isn't useful.

To a scientist, it is a mortal sin to compare animals to people. It's called anthropomorphism – imagining animals as being just like us, with emotions and individual personalities. In this book, I invite you to join me in this mortal sin, to put yourself in the place of an animal. You might be a bat whose eyes hurt under bright light, or a springtail that can jump unexpectedly into the sky. Because, you see, I have no doubt that these animals have their own individual feelings and passions.

We will try to get inside their heads, to think about how we could make a better world for them, from their point of view.

Saving the planet can be a little overwhelming. Where do we start? My suggestion is to pick one animal every year. And over the year, try everything you can to attract it to your home. Make a plan like the one at the back of this book, and fill it in as you go along. And whatever you do will have effects on many other species. For example, you might build a pond for newts, but hedgehogs might drink from it. Or you could plant some flowers for bees, and bats may feed over them. So be prepared for the unexpected. And be patient – it took newts four years to move into our pond, and some species of bat can take a while to try out bat boxes. Do what you can, and next year try a different species.

A lot of the suggestions involve doing nothing – for instance, letting the grass grow. Remember, anywhere can be a nature reserve, from a giant farm to an apartment balcony. You can be a voice for nature. Just put yourself in their skins.

Give it a go!

WHAT LIES BENEATH

People usually don't take much interest in the animals beneath our feet. If we can't see it, then we tend not to think about it. But life underground is crucially important to life above ground. Soil ecology is closely related to plant and animal ecology.

What *is* in the soil? There's a micro food web of bacteria, fungi and small animals, all leading busy lives beneath your feet. Creatures beneath you right now include nematodes, protozoa, springtails, beetles and earthworms.

EARTHWORMS

Earthworms are amazing. They drag stuff from above the soil down below the earth, bringing nutrients deep into the ground. Their tunnels aerate the ground, and their casts (earthworm poo!) are particularly important for soil health. There are up to 10,000 types of microbes in these casts, and these nourish plants and help fight plant diseases. There are many YouTube videos on bioturbation (earthworms tunnelling through soil), and they're strangely relaxing to watch! Grab yourself a cuppa, light a scented candle and switch on some bioturbation. You will feel much better afterwards.

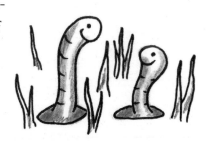

Activities for children

- See how many earthworms you have! Dig a 20cm by 20cm (by 20cm deep) pit. That's about the length of a shovel. Carefully pull the soil apart. Put it all in a tray and count the earthworms, then return them to their soil.

SPRINGTAILS

If you have ever pulled a Christmas cracker, you may have found a little plastic toy that springs into the air when you push its rear end. The animal equivalent of this is the spring-tail – they've been described as the Tigger of the insect world. Springtails have a forked structure attached to their belly called a furcula, and when they need a quick getaway, they release it and bounce high into the air.

It looks as if they are popping away randomly, with little sense of direction, but in fact they have a small tube by their back legs called a collophore, which they use to direct their spring. When they are not springing around, they use this collophore to groom themselves. Their jump is enormous: up to 300 times the size of the insect. That would be equivalent to people being able to spring over skyscrapers!

wheee

I have often thought about what animal trait I would like to have if I was able to magically conjure up powers. I think I'd like a furcula. And a collophore, so I would look good too when I suddenly arrived at my destination.

DUNG BEETLES

Dung beetles are essential in our fight against poo. They also look spectacular, with shiny little bodies. There are several different types – you have probably seen wildlife films of 'rollers'. These tiny beetles push large balls of poo. In the films, they are usually dwarfed by an enormous poo, and are pushing it up a hill, until they reach their burrow, where they push it in. They have enormous strength and perseverance, and watching them makes the rest of us feel very inadequate.

These beetles are not found in Ireland. But we have 'tunnellers' here. These dig tunnels, fill them with dung and lay eggs in it. Moving the dung around also helps to disperse seeds, as well as bringing nutrients underground, which benefits plants. A third type of dung beetle is the 'dweller', which breeds in surface dung.

What would we do without them? Moving dung around clearly gets it out of our way. Bringing it underground brings nutrients to plants, improves the soil structure and gets rid of parasites that could reinfect animals. The underground dung also increases the activity of underground microbes. Dung beetles are also an important foodstuff for bats. There is a concern that when wormers are used in cattle and horses, dung beetles can be killed by the chemical in the cowpat. And without dung beetles, we are all in deep shit.

Building healthy soil

- Don't allow soil to be bare. When soil is bare, soil erosion takes place. If you have a gap somewhere, cover it with a green manure – basically throw seeds in to cover the soil. On farms, oats can be used to cover fields; in gardens, you can use comfrey or mustard. Use whatever you like, but don't leave the soil naked!

- Try not to disturb the soil with digging or ploughing. Our local primary school came to visit once and calculated the amount of soil lost in a one-hectare field that I had recently ploughed. I can't remember the exact weight, but it equated to the weight of 26 primary schoolchildren. They all rolled down the hill field to make the point. No-dig or light tilling is the way to go.

- Stop compacting the soil. When you walk or drive heavy machinery over the soil, it squashes everything beneath, and makes it harder for small creatures to wriggle through. So, make paths through your garden, and stick to them. And avoid using heavy machinery.

- Start a compost bin. Earthworms will love you for it. Just throw in your uncooked food waste, paper and cardboard, and forget about it. You may end up with lovely compost. Or, like mine, the stuff will vanish, magically disappearing into the ground, dragged away by earthworms.

- Stop concreting and hard surfacing. We are losing vast amounts of soil every year to hard surfacing, often for our cars. We need to find ways to allow soil to breathe. There are alternatives to paving your garden to park your car. You could go retro – in the 1970s, my neighbours all paved the areas along the wheel tracks of their cars. Grass was free to grow in between, underneath the car body. If you want it to look more stylish, you can use a lattice of concrete. This looks like a chess board, where there is a square of concrete, then one of grass, then one of concrete, and so on. Or you can use a geogrid mesh, which is strong enough to drive a car on, while sitting on your lawn. An additional advantage to all of this is that flooding is reduced when water can soak through the earth. And with the increase in rainfall due to climate change, we need our gardens to protect our homes.

- Only use animal wormers if you need them. Most vets will carry out analysis of dung, to let you know if your horse or donkey needs worming. Have this done before you routinely worm your animals. They may not need it.

LARGER MAMMALS

BADGERS

I have watched wild badgers for many years, and was lucky enough to encounter one up close when I worked on a project in Dublin. A flood defence wall was being built along a river, and a badger sett was along the river too. The new wall would cut through the sett, so the decision was made to build an artificial sett. We would trap the badgers, move them to the new sett and feed them for a month or two. We would then release them and allow them back to their old sett when the work was finished.

The badgers were very resistant to being trapped. Night after night we sat for hours, watching cats, foxes and everything else go into the traps. And then one night, Michael appeared. He was a young badger, with a bad gash on his head. He had clearly been in a fight with another badger – or with a car. He sat quietly in the badger trap until he saw us, and then, in total despair, he covered his eyes with his paws and made loud sobbing sounds. Honestly, he looked like a large, sad, furry toy.

When we moved him to the new sett area, I opened the cage. But like a kidnap victim with Stockholm syndrome, he refused to leave and huddled in the corner. How would we get him out of the cage? I took a stick and started gently pushing him out. He removed his paws, looked at me with a clear look of 'please stop torturing me!', then placed his paws back over his face and resumed sobbing. He was like a child who is so upset that they can't catch their breath. Poor Michael.

We crept away and waited, and finally he shot out of the cage, and down to the new sett. It was several days before he was brave enough to come out for food.

BADGER SETTS

One hole in the ground looks much like another hole in the ground when you are trying to identify mammal underground homes, but if you can fit a football inside the hole, you probably have a badger sett. If you do find a sett, keep it a secret. Badgers have been persecuted for many years by badger baiters, and traps and snares are still set today by these cruel people.

There are several different types of sett, and they can be enormous. The main sett is like the ancestral home. It has been passed down through the generations, and badgers are extremely attached to it. They often bring in pieces of plastic bag to line it with, making it waterproof and giving it a strange interior design aesthetic. My husband found one that was lined with hundreds of Coca-Cola bottles. Main setts are big, with lots of entrances, and are used most of the time. Many setts have indoor toilet areas.

The annex sett is like the granny flat, with a smaller number of entrances, generally used when badgers want to have a quick night away from the relatives. The outlier sett has just one entrance and is further away – a bit like a holiday cottage, when they plan to stay out all night and they're far from home. Of course, these sett descriptions can intermingle. Just like ourselves, badgers move around and change the design of their homes.

As badgers extend their setts, they drag out a lot of soil. They use their hind legs to kick the soil out, moving backwards in their tunnels. The soil that is dumped at the entrance is called a spoil heap. So, in addition to the football-sized hole, you may find some mounds of soil – and also some dried grass and bedding.

Badgers are exceptionally clean animals and, like myself, they often drag out their bedding to air it. I hang my duvet on the line, but they spread their bed around in the sunshine. This cleans it and gets rid of parasites. The same process gets rid of dust mites in my duvet. Then they inspect their bedding, judging whether it has to be thrown out or can be reused, before dragging it back into their chamber.

Tunnels are usually semi-circular, with corridors leading off them at sharp angles. The tunnels lead to chambers, which are a squashed oval shape, about half a metre high and wide. The sett must be warm enough to protect the badger (some research shows that the temperature inside the sett is around 11°C) while allowing enough oxygen through so the animal can breathe. The chambers must also fit bedding, plus another badger sometimes. It must all be a little squashed.

Sometimes tunnels where a badger has died are closed off, providing an underground, in-house burial chamber. Later on, when only a skeleton remains, spring cleaning is done and the skeleton is tossed out with the soil. If you ever find a skull, and are wondering what it is, lift it up (wear gloves!). If the jaw remains attached, it is a badger skull. Their lower jaws are attached by bone. You are probably moving your jaw around right now, as I am, wondering how our jaws are attached. Unlike those of badgers, our lower jaws are only attached by muscle. Without this muscle, our lower jaw would fall off. Now that's something to chew on!

Two captive badgers were recorded building their own heating system. They carried straw and hay to a chamber within their sett and allowed it to ferment. It reached 38°C, and the badgers would move closer to it when they were cold. They did this several years in a row.

Who does the housework in the sett? Not surprisingly, it seems that the parents do most of the work, digging and carrying bedding around. Older males and females spend a lot of time keeping their home clean, while the sett is used by the whole group. It's just like Christmas in most households.

We built an artificial sett at home. There are many designs on the internet for homemade sett design, so it might be worth giving this a try. Four years later, badgers still have not moved in – but they have started to mark the sett with latrines (little toilets) outside the entrance. Perhaps they are trying to tell me what they think of my sett! After all, if you had a perfectly good ancestral home, why would you move into a home built by another species? If badgers built a home for me, I might appreciate the toilet areas and heating systems. But I wouldn't enjoy the tiny rooms and long corridors, and my ancestors being sealed into the walls. Meanwhile, my badgers visit our sett regularly. They check out my grand design and have some peanuts and a poo. As humans, we are probably getting something wrong when we build artificial setts.

BADGERS AND BOVINE TB

Badgers suffer from tuberculosis, or TB. The million-dollar question is whether they can transmit TB to cattle. I believe it is very unlikely that a cow will catch TB from a badger. And here is the science behind my opinion:

TB in cattle is usually found in their lungs. For a badger to infect a cow, it would have to come within 1.5 metres of the cow, and ideally be breathing at it. Sadly, we all now understand about social distancing and aerosol droplet dispersal. And lots of interesting science has taken place in Ireland, looking at badgers and cattle, and their social distances.

A project led by National Parks and Wildlife Service (NPWS) Divisional Ecologist Enda Mullen spent three years tracking badgers in the Wicklow countryside. Forty badgers, from 12 social groups, had radio collars placed around their necks. Then enthusiastic NPWS staff and volunteers from Trinity College Dublin plotted 12,500 movements of the badgers as they roamed the countryside.

How would the badgers meet the cattle? Might a badger be lured into a farmyard by some spilled grain, coming into contact with livestock housed in sheds? This study proved otherwise. The badgers tended to avoid farmyards – and particularly farmyards with cattle. If they visited farmyards at all, they tended to visit equestrian farmyards and disused farmyards. But most badgers kept away even from these. A single individual badger (which the researchers christened 'Violet') seemed to like a trip to the horses, and went to visit a stable several times, but most other badgers kept far away from all livestock, and were even scared of visiting disused farmyards.

A second study, undertaken by Declan O'Mahoney in Northern Ireland, confirmed that badgers avoid cattle. Declan works with the Agri-Food and Biosciences Institute in Belfast, and his approach was slightly different. He placed proximity collars on 58 cattle and 11 badgers in a bovine TB (bTB) hotspot in Northern Ireland. If the badgers and cattle came within 2 metres of each other (close enough to share a breath), the collars would emit a pulse. This would be plotted via GPS. In addition, motion-sensor cameras were placed all over the farmyards to video anything that moved.

The results were amazing. There were over 350,000 interactions between cattle and cattle. There were 11,774 interactions between badger and badger. Clearly, you hang out with your own species. And there were no interactions between cattle and badgers. Zero!

So, is TB being transmitted by badgers? And if so, how? The researchers looked at water troughs. But badgers and cattle did not use water troughs concurrently. In fact, badgers rarely used water troughs at all. So, the researchers turned their attention to the farmyards. In a mammoth undertaking, they recorded 500,000 hours of video at farmyards and analysed the results. That must have been a really tedious job! The visiting animals recorded most were feral cats, some of which were in poor condition. Farm cats play an important role in rodent control, but can also be carriers of TB, and any animal in poor condition is more susceptible to disease. Mice and rats were also seen on camera, and, very rarely, an individual badger (perhaps a friend of Violet's?) visited a meal shed for a few minutes. Most other badgers kept away – and all badgers avoided the cattle sheds.

Cattle are large, sometimes dangerous and scarily frisky. It seems that badgers are aware of this and keep far away from them. However, the badger continues to be blamed for transmission of the disease to cattle. Over 100,000 badgers (some pregnant and nursing) have been killed under the TB eradication programme, and yet the rates of bovine TB in Ireland have increased. It's time to stop scapegoating the badger, and support farmers in finding the real underlying causes of this disease.

A YEAR IN THE LIFE OF A BADGER

Badgers have their young in early spring, and female badgers come into heat soon after birth. They often become pregnant again before their first cub is weaned. Any mother of so called 'Irish twins' will know how this feels. If the badger doesn't become pregnant again, she will continue to come into heat about every 28 days.

Amazingly, although badgers may mate in spring, the blastocyst – the collection of fertilised cells – swims around in the female uterus for several months. While the blastocyst is swimming about, the female can come into heat again, and another blastocyst can form. This is called superfetation, and is very unusual in mammals. One blastocyst may be a different age and size to another. Lyndsey Stuart in TCD has worked out how it happens. All the blastocysts finally implant into the mother's womb in wintertime. So, though cubs are born together, they can have different fathers. Female badgers don't put all their eggs in one basket!

The male tries his best to seduce the female. He struts around the outside of the sett, purring and generally sounding attractive. If that fails, he uses scent glands, like DIY aftershave, to create that special smell. Mating can take from 1 to 90 minutes. The aftershave clearly works wonders.

There are often 2 to 3 cubs in a litter, and they are adorable when born, with small pink noses. They start to wean at about 12 weeks, but may continue to feed and generally hang around with their mother for many months. Sadly, as with most wild animals, at least half the badgers born don't make it to their second year.

Many badgers stay around their group forever, and it was thought that this could make them inbred. However, DNA analysis is showing that this isn't the case. At least 50% of the cubs born in a group have parentage from outside the group. Badgers are clearly sneaking away in the night for some scent marking and purring in other setts.

Badgers can live for up to 15 years in the wild. Although they don't hibernate, they often spend long periods underground, tucked away in their setts in the winter months.

Attracting badgers to your area

- Badgers often wander along defined paths and tracks. You will notice that there is a track through the grass, and you may see coarse hair caught on a wire fence or footprints of a badger in mud. Put out food along these tracks in winter. Badgers like to eat cat and dog food, peanuts, fruit and even cooked potatoes. It is also worth putting out water in frosty or hot spells.

Activities for children

- Look for a badger footprint. This is best done in spring in muddy areas. You will need moulding plaster for the next part. Take a cardboard Tetra Pak-type container from your recycle bin. Pull both ends out of the container and place it over the footprint. Mix some moulding plaster with water. Pour the plaster into the container, up to a centimetre or two, and leave it for half an hour. Remove the container and, hey presto! You have made a lovely plaster-cast of a badger footprint.

FOXES

If you are out late at night, and hear a bloodcurdling scream, you are hearing a fox (hopefully!). Foxes are amazing – they look like dogs but behave like cats, and you can see them everywhere.

When I was young, I used to help out with a wildlife group in Blanchardstown in Dublin. They had some small sheds and cages and ran a wildlife hospital. One lunchtime, I opened a shed to find utter devastation. Food, cages and bedding were everywhere, while a rook squawked

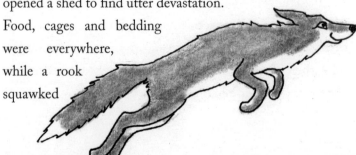

miserably in his cage. Sitting peacefully in his own cage was a fox. I eventually found a small hole in the fox's cage. The fox, which had been hit by a car and knocked unconscious, had suddenly come back to life, clambered out of his cage, trashed the place and terrified the rook, then climbed back into his cage and fallen asleep. I began to believe that foxes could do anything.

FOXES, HENS AND LAMBS

How do you keep stock safe when the fox is so agile? I myself have lost hens to foxes, and in fact was in my chicken pen once with a fox. He was so fast, I felt as if I was moving in slow motion, slowly shouting, yelling and waving my arms, as he sped by.

But there are fox-proof pens. By far the best is any type of electric fence. Specialised chicken electric fences are sold, which have an electrified wire mesh. These are fantastic – one shock and your fox will not return. And the mesh is easily moved to allow the hens onto new grass. With a traditional hen pen, a line of ordinary electric fencing wire can be run near the bottom of the pen. This will also work. Remember that foxes can dig, so if you have a traditional hen pen, make sure it has a 'skirt' of wire running along the base to prevent foxes burrowing in.

Although foxes may take lambs, work by Ray Hewson with the University of Aberdeen finds that they mostly take carcases or lambs that are very weak. Many farmers nowadays bring their sheep indoors for lambing, which keeps them safe and makes it easier to monitor the births.

A YEAR IN THE LIFE OF A FOX

Foxes are omnivores. They will eat rats, mice and rabbits, as well as berries, fruit and earthworms. They also love eating our leftovers, and you may have seen them eating a bag of dropped chips or raiding a bin. In doing this, they are providing a free refuse-disposal system, not to mention a pest-control service, eating both our dropped rubbish and the rats drawn to it.

Scent is everything to foxes, and they communicate a lot through smell. They have scent glands under their tails, by their anal gland, and even in their feet. Foxes have very, very smelly feet. Unfortunately, because of this, hounds can track their paths easily. They also leave scent trails in their urine, like dogs. This marks their territory and gives a lot of information on the individual fox. Fox toilets are basically the Facebook of fox lives, announcing who the fox is with, and where she's going.

Foxes live underground in dens. Unlike badgers, who really love a tidy home, foxes are messy, with bits of beds and bones thrown everywhere. It's just like a teenager's bedroom. Vixens tend to share a territory, although they may not live together. Normally, the male fox mates with just one vixen, the dominant female, and brings her food when she has cubs. However, in stressful situations, when it's likely that the foxes will get killed, the male may mate with more than one female. It's just like people with wartime romances. This was first noticed in urban areas, where foxes are likely to be killed by cars. It may also be the reason that fox numbers have been found to increase in the countryside after wintertime fox hunting.

When the vixen is in heat, she screams in a really spooky

way. Irish people have imaginative minds, and thought this was the scream of the banshee, a long-haired hag, dressed in a dark cloak, who foretold the death of someone from your household. Terrifying stuff! In fact, it's an attractive love song to a male fox. The vixen is pregnant for 52 days, and usually has 4 to 5 cubs, which look like teddy bears, with brown fur and rounded ears. The male brings food for the vixen, and other vixens may act as babysitters. The cubs are completely dependent on milk for the first three weeks, then weaning begins. The young continue to suckle for another six weeks or so.

When the cubs start to emerge above ground, they are absolutely clueless about danger, and you may get quite close to them. They play a lot, barging about and knocking each other over. This tests their strength.

In October, the young disperse. The vixens tend to stay around their home territory, while the males roam further afield. Like ourselves, they can move home for a variety of reasons. They may be pushed out of their home range if there is not enough food, shelter, or other resources – just like many unemployed young Irish people, who had to emigrate during our last economic crash. Or they might be pulled to a new place by the attentions of a young vixen.

Foxes can live up to 14 years in captivity, but generally live about 3 years in the wild. Resist the temptation to 'tame' a local fox. Don't try to feed it from your hand or encourage it to befriend you. Not all people are as kind as you – for their own safety, foxes must always associate humans with danger.

Attracting foxes to your area

- Put out food, especially in the winter and in very dry weather. In dry weather, the ground is hard, so it is difficult to find earthworms. Foxes will eat lots of stuff – dog food (dry and wet), cheese and fruit are favourites. In theory, foxes will eat unsalted peanuts, but they never touch the ones I put out for mine! Leave out fresh water for them in dry spells.

  Plant some dense shrubs that foxes can hide in. Foxes also can den under sheds and woodpiles, but don't like open space.

Foxy activities for children

- Foxes are smelly. Take the kids for a walk and ask them to smell for foxes. Small children, still in the 'poo is wonderful' stage, can hunt for fox scats. Fox poo is a little like dog poo, but is twisty and pointed. Wearing gloves, use a stick to break apart the poo. In it you will find traces of whatever the fox ate – seeds, hair and perhaps small bones. You will now have a map of fox crossings and an idea of its diet. This may sound like an odd way to spend an afternoon, but your child may grow up to become a zoologist.

RABBITS AND HARES
IRISH HARES

The Irish hare is an amazing-looking animal, larger than a rabbit and with really powerful hind legs. It makes a 'form' – a type of bed in a shallow pit, made with tall grass or rushes, where it can shelter from the wind and hide from its enemies. Its brown fur blends into the earth. It mainly uses concealment as protection from predators, but if disturbed it can run very quickly (up to 70km per hour), twisting and turning to escape.

You will often see hares in March and April, charging about and boxing each other. They may look 'as mad as a March hare', but what you're witnessing is sexual harassment. The males attempt to mate with unwilling females, and the females box them. The females are generally larger than the males, with a strong punch, but the males are persistent. Occasionally the males box each other too. This is the easiest time of year to see hares, as they are so focussed on chasing, boxing and mating that they forget you are watching.

Females have 2 to 3 litters a year, with 1 to 4 young, which are called leverets. The mother hare knows that she will draw attention to her young, lying above ground in their form, so she leaves them alone by day, returning just at dusk to feed them. The young drink their mother's milk for three weeks. Leverets are very susceptible to attack from predators, and it is estimated that only one in five young survive to adulthood. If they survive, they can live up to 9 years.

I used to work in Blanchardstown Hospital in Dublin. It was an old TB hospit balconies stretching out onto parkland. The patients were often wheeled outside and spent many hours watching hares in the sunshine. A lovely way to feel better.

A study undertaken by the NPWS in 2019

showed that there are about 3.19 hares per square km in Ireland. A study in 2007 had shown that there were 7.44 hares per square km. This is clearly a huge drop in hare numbers. However, survey techniques and equipment has improved, so this might account for some of the variation in numbers. The 2019 study used 596 camera traps and recorded about 106,026 hours (about 12 years!) of visual data. What a fantastic level of detail. And hares can be difficult to record on remote camera. We have one shot from a camera on our farm where the hare appears to be pulling faces. It did a really good impression of a deer! On our farm, the numbers of hares have also dropped.

In Ireland, hares are taken for coursing, both legally and illegally, and now are challenged by rabbit haemorrhagic disease. In years gone by, it was thought that the soul of your grandmother lived in the Irish hare. It looks to me as if granny is in danger.

BROWN HARES

The brown hare is not native to Ireland, but was introduced here in the nineteenth century for hare coursing. Unluckily for it, hare coursers considered that the brown hare runs in a very exciting way. I would also run in a very exciting way if I was being chased by a bloodthirsty pack of hounds.

The brown hare is slightly bigger than the Irish hare, with longer ears that have black tips. It may pose some threat to the Irish hare population, being larger and presumably stronger. It is mostly found in mid Ulster and west Tyrone. In research in Queen's University in Belfast, brown hares accounted for up to 62% of hares found in mid Ulster.

Do Irish hares and brown hares breed together? Well, they are definitely considering it. There are many tales of boxing matches between brown and Irish hares. However, no young have yet been found.

Rabbits in Ireland have suffered from myxomatosis in the past, and the disease seems to have jumped species to the brown hare in England. So far, there are no signs of myxomatosis in any hares in Ireland, but this is being closely monitored.

If you are a farmer and cut hay or silage, start the cutting in the centre of the field and mow from the centre to the edges. This will allow young hares and other animals to escape to the edges of the field. Otherwise, they will become trapped in an 'island' of grass at the centre of the field and may be killed by the tractor.

RABBITS

Peter, our pet rabbit, lives free in our garden, where he regularly battles with wild rabbits, which run out of the fields to argue with him. Like snarling dogs on each side of a gate, the rabbits threaten each other and there have been a few bloody noses. But anyone who has owned a rabbit will tell you that these animals have huge personalities, packed into their small, hopping bodies.

Rabbits were introduced to Ireland by the Normans and have become widespread. You will find them almost everywhere they can burrow, with a few exceptions. They don't like very wet land, or coniferous forests. Their ideal place to eat is on shortish grass near bramble or hedgerow. Then they have a safe place to hide if they need to make a quick getaway.

Rabbits look like the cutest animals on earth, with huge eyes on the sides of their heads. With these eyes, they can see almost 360 degrees. They also have a good sense of smell, and their enormous ears provide them with excellent hearing. All of this is necessary when almost everything wants to eat you!

I wish I had the teeth of a rabbit – it would save a fortune in dentist bills. Rabbits' teeth grow constantly – about 2mm per week – so they are continually replacing teeth that are worn down from grazing on hard objects. Imagine being able to happily graze a twig from a tree. It would make a great segment in cookery programmes. Rabbits and hares are classed as lagomorphs. All lagomorphs have a second set of incisor teeth, called peg teeth, behind their front ones. This gives them that Bugs Bunny grin!

There is a 'yeuch' side to the diets of rabbits and hares. Grasses and heathers digest in their cecum, basically a big fermentation vat beyond their small intestine. Fibre is broken down, and a gooey ball of B-vitamins and proteins is created. But how does it get back into the small intestine for absorption? You've guessed it. The rabbit poos a mucus-covered ball and eats it immediately. Hey presto, vitamin B. It may sound awful, but perhaps if we could do this too, we would be able to eat grass, re-ingest poo and be a lot less likely to end up in hospital, having our appendix removed.

A YEAR IN THE LIFE OF A RABBIT

Rabbits breed – well, like rabbits. They can have up to 45 young a year. The more dominant females have better burrows, and their young are more likely to survive. The female can have 5 to 10 young, called kittens, in her underground warren. The young are truly defenceless, born blind and hairless. They open their eyes at around 10 days old, and wean at around 18 days old.

With such high numbers of rabbits being born, why aren't we overrun with them? To start with, everything wants to eat them. They are a big prey item for buzzards, foxes and stoats. Then there is the weather. In summertime, there is plenty to eat and rabbit numbers can reach up to 40 per hectare. But in winter, there is less food, and numbers drop down to about 15 per hectare. Agrichemicals can also poison them, both directly (when they eat them) and indirectly, when weeds are sprayed. These weeds would have been their food for the winter.

And then there is disease. Rabbits are social creatures and share underground spaces, and disease spreads easily here. Myxomatosis is a rabbit disease that was deliberately introduced into France by a person who wanted to reduce the numbers of rabbits on his estate. Perhaps he should have thought of a kinder way to do this. Myxomatosis spread wildly through Europe, killing around 90% of rabbits. The sick rabbits have swollen eyes and become immunocompromised, thus allowing other illnesses to kill them. Many die from pneumonia.

With all the threats to rabbits, it is just as well that they breed so well. Ninety-five percent of rabbit kittens die within their first year. But the kitten has a better chance of survival if it is born early in the year, as it has time to grow a little before winter comes. Rabbits live about 1.5 years in the wild, but can live up to 10 years in captivity. It's a dangerous life. If I was reincarnated as an animal, I definitely would not choose to be a rabbit!

RABBIT HAEMORRHAGIC DISEASE

This disease of rabbits and hares is a serious threat to populations in Ireland. It came from China in 1984, and a variant of it, RHD2, spread through Europe and into France. It was first recognised in Ireland in 2016, and as I write, has now been found in twelve counties. It is spreading quickly, so if you find a dead hare or rabbit, please contact the National Parks and Wildlife Service.

Thankfully, this disease does not transmit to humans. But it kills rabbits and hares, causing paralysis and bleeding from the mouth and eyes. It is easily transmitted, carried on clothing and shoes, and has been found in pet rabbits too. Luckily, there is now a vaccine for pet rabbits, but our wild pals are at serious risk.

Attracting hares and rabbits to your area
- Let grass grow long. Encourage the local park or school to provide some dog-free areas of long grass, where hares can rest or breed.
- Help hares by joining the Irish Council Against Blood Sports.

Activities for children

- Play 'The Fox and the Rabbit': Scatter hula hoops around a grassy area. Two children are foxes and must chase and catch the other children. The other children are safe in their burrows (the hula hoops), but must visit each burrow. The game of 'tag' begins!

STOATS

You may have seen a street performer doing tricks with a long piece of fur, which bounces around attached to an unseen string. Kids often use it to play with kittens. This crazy bit of fur is the nylon equivalent of the stoat.

Stoats seem to live in some other weird space-time continuum. They are unbelievably fast, and will leave you trailing behind, wondering, 'What did I just see?' They bound along, looking like a dancing elastic band with enormous energy.

They live in most types of habitat and can even live in cities. I know of one living happily beside Malahide Castle in Dublin. They look like a weasel, but have brown fur with a white belly, and a black line on the boundary of their white fur. They always have black at tip of their tails.

The Irish stoat is its own subspecies, and so it is important to protect it. Females are much smaller than males. Stoats must eat at least 20% of their body weight each day. Their diet includes rats, mice, birds' eggs and shrews,

35

and they can even swim and grab fish. But their favourite food is rabbits, which can make up up to 50% of their diet. Rabbits are cream cakes and chocolate bars all rolled into one for stoats. But when rabbits die of myxomatosis, stoat numbers also crash. Stoats have also found a use for the coat of the rabbit – we have found stoat dens lined with strange wall hangings of rabbit fur. Like old-fashioned tapestries, these keep the den cosy and warm.

Stoats are agile and can climb trees. They are small, but strong for their size. We left a dead hen in some hedgerow on our farm and filmed whatever came to eat it. We got lots of footage of a stoat pulling and dragging at the hen, but the hen was too big for it to move. The stoat eventually gave up and left it, and a mouse came and collected all the hen's feathers for its nest.

Stoats den in rabbit, rat and mouse burrows – sometimes having eaten the original resident! They also live in piles of sticks and stones. On our farm, they live in a gap in an old stone wall by a river.

A YEAR IN THE LIFE OF A STOAT

For some unknown reason, stoats are heavier in the south of Ireland than they are in the north. They mate in summer, but do not implant the egg and become pregnant until the following spring. They have their young around April, having 5 to 12 babies, which reach adult size by September. Stoats can live up to ten years, with an average lifespan of around 3 years.

Most travel around 250 metres per day (though that figure isn't exactly correct, as stoats live a three-dimensional life, going up and down trees, as well as running along the ground).

We know very little about stoats, partly because they are difficult to locate. How do you find a really fast, small animal that seems to move in all directions at once? And if you find it, how do you fit a radio collar on it? The animal is long and narrow, and the collar will just slide off. Camera traps can film them, but stoats are so fast, they are usually gone before the camera triggers. Sometimes tunnels are put out, with a type of gluey tape inside that traps hairs of an animal as it goes through. Again, this is difficult, and the hair often requires DNA testing to be sure of the species – it can all become incredibly expensive.

The Vincent Wildlife Trust have come up with a great way of monitoring stoats. They realised that stoats are incredibly curious when they find tunnels. You would be too if your dinner was always hidden inside one! So, they build a stoat curiosity box, called a 'Mostela' – basically a wooden box with a camera inside and a plastic drainpipe sticking out. Stoats find this fascinating, and you can spend many happy hours on YouTube watching life inside the Mostela, with stoats running through the drainpipe and checking out the box.

Attracting stoats to your garden
• Piles of logs, rocks and stones give stoats somewhere to hide. And they will keep the local rat population down! If you are on a farm, remember that stone walls are great places for stoats.

Activities for children
• Build a Mostela, and see what comes to visit!

PINE MARTENS

Our farm has trail cameras everywhere. Imagine our delight when we saw our first pine marten in 2018. How exciting. Twenty years of surveying, planting woods, building ponds and laying hedgerows and at last a pine marten comes onto our farm.

Bad news came next, as the pine marten managed to get into our chicken shed and killed all my hens. It was awful. But several days later, the pine marten was back – and she brought two adorable pine marten kittens with her. Her apology was accepted! She may have killed the hens, but she was just trying to feed her family. And the kittens were amazing, jumping on and off a plastic bag with a fright every time it crackled.

We now have a better hen pen, and we feed the pine marten every night. It has a penchant for fat balls, and we have some amazing footage of the pine marten carrying a fat ball in its mouth like a giant gobstopper.

A group of pine martens is called a richesse, which is the medieval word for richness, and I definitely think that life is richer if you have a pine marten calling to your home. In fact, the pine marten was given that name because of the

fabulous richness of its long, bushy fur. The coat looks wonderfully warm, but in reality, it isn't great at holding heat. The marten has a long body, which also increases heat loss, and it is a lean, muscular animal, with low amounts of body fat. The lack of fat also means that it doesn't like cold temperatures.

Thankfully, it has a long, bushy tail, which it can wrap around itself like a living fur coat. And the pine marten has a great strategy for staying warm in wintertime – it stays in bed. Studies from Andrzej Zatewski in Poland found pine martens being active for just 2.8 hours per day in winter, as opposed to over 12 hours a day in summertime. They may have the right idea – perhaps we should all be pulling that duvet back over our heads in the winter.

The pine marten moves like a ballerina, with a floaty, springy gait. Its long tail may be used to add a spring to its gait, and is very useful for climbing in trees, acting like the pole that tightrope walkers use to balance themselves. The pine marten also has amazing hind feet, with flexible ankles that can turn 180°. Even the best ballet dancers and tightrope walkers would find that impossible.

Underneath the pine martens' neck, below its heart-shaped face, is a creamy white- to orange-coloured bib. I have heard that each marten has an individual pattern to its bib, and that it is possible to tell individuals apart. Our pine marten always has his face so stuffed with food that we never get a look at the bib, but I imagine we have one individual who comes to visit, night after night.

It can be difficult to tell the age of a pine marten, but, like ourselves, their teeth tend to get worse as they get older. The teeth wear down, and an older pine marten may have gaps where teeth have fallen out. In the absence of pine marten dentistry, some pine martens starve when their teeth are lost.

If you find a dead pine marten, you can age it by looking in its mouth. If it has bright, shiny, sharp, pointed teeth, it's probably a young one. If it is looking a little gummy, you have an older animal.

In Irish folklore, Queen Maedhbh had a pet pine marten, which she wore around her neck. Cú Chulainn killed it with a slingshot. No wonder she hated him!

A YEAR IN THE LIFE OF A PINE MARTEN

Trees are particularly important to pine martens, as they spend up to 90% of their time resting in them. They really need holes in trees to get cosy in, and trees with suitable holes tend to be over 100 years old. This is a problem in Ireland, as many of our trees are younger. Many old trees with holes in them are classed as dangerous and are felled. Then the trees are 'tidied away' and all deadwood is removed or mulched.

Queen's University put radio collars on 20 wild pine martens and followed them to see where they went. Their first choice was always to den in living or dead trees in forests. When this was impossible, they used hedgerows and buildings – bringing them into conflict with humans. Studies have shown that pine martens can have different home ranges, but often have a core range of 2km, where they spend most of their time.

I really love fruit and berries, and at all times have an extra freezer full of blackcurrants and two cupboards full of jam. I may have been a pine marten in a past life. Recent research by Áine Lynch and Yvonne McCann looked at the diet of pine martens in Killarney National Park. They found that fruit was the foodstuff they ate the most. However, they also eat small rodents, insects, amphibians, birds and nuts.

How can we find pine martens? Pine martens hate getting their feet wet in mud, so it can be difficult to find their footprints. It is also difficult to see a wild pine marten, as you will see just a flash of bounding fur, which leaves you wondering, 'Was that a cat?' But luckily their scats (poo) are easy to find. They tend to poo in an obvious place – along the trunk of a fallen tree, on an obvious branch or on a forest path. The scat looks like a cross between a slug and a walnut whip – it's mushy and wobbly, and you can't fail to notice it. The pine marten moves its hips while pooing (we don't know why), which gives the scat its odd shape. The poo also smells lovely.

Pine martens are slow to breed, have few young, take care of them for a long time, and live to a ripe old age. A little like ourselves. Animals tend either to use a strategy of having lots of young, weaning them fast and sending them off on their own; or the opposite strategy of having a few young and really taking care of them. It's quality versus quantity. A lack of parental involvement, fast weaning and large litters means that most of the young will die. However, some will live. But having a small number of young is also risky – the panda is almost at the point of extinction because of this strategy.

The pine marten generally only has 2 to 3 kittens. The males are often 3 years old before they become sexually mature, and the females are 2 years old before they can breed. This is a long teenage phase, when they can hang around and even share dens with their mum.

They mate in summertime, and the blastocyst implants between February and March. They seem to decide on exactly the right time to become pregnant, based on the amount of food available and the daylight length. Studies show that if lots of mice are available for food, the young will be born earlier.

The mum finds a den around February, and is pregnant for 30 days. Babies are generally born in April. The kits stay in their dens for around 30 days, and when they finally come out, they are really clumsy. It's like toddlers learning to walk, but unfortunately their home is up a tree. As there are no stair gates for pine martens, accidents frequently happen. So, around this time, the mum may decide to move home to a safer place, such as a tree which is easier to climb. The kits may hang around with mum for many months, before going off to find a new territory of their own.

Studies on dead pine martens on roads showed that many were aged from 9 to 11 years. Quite an age for such a small mammal!

One problem with pine martens is that they are likely to kill hens – your hens must be protected if you have pine martens around. It is a horrible experience to arrive at your chicken pen to find a lot of dead animals. What makes it worse is the seemingly mindless waste of life. Often the entire flock is dead, with only one or two hens gone. However, if left alone, the pine marten would continue to return and take away the dead hens to store for future eating. It's like doing all your weekly shop with just one small shopping bag – ideally you would do it over several days with many journeys. We shouldn't blame the pine marten too much – in Ireland, people waste over one million tonnes of food each year.

To save your hens, electricity is your friend! Running an electric fence around the hen pen, or using purpose-made electric hen netting, really works well. Pine martens can dig and climb, so the pen must be fully enclosed, with wire running at ground level along the base to prevent any animal from digging in. The Vincent Wildlife Trust also recommend using corrugated steel along the sides of the pen to prevent the hens and pine marten from seeing each other. The VWT have done extensive research with gamekeepers to design the perfect pine marten-proof pen. The design of this can be found on *pinemarten.ie*.

Pine martens ideally nest in trees that are over 100 years old, with lovely holes and crevices. Sadly, such trees are frequently felled. These trees should be made safe and retained, even if they are dead. The hotel Cabra Castle in Kingscourt, Co. Cavan, has saved some wonderful ancient and dead trees, chopping branches to ensure they are safe from falling, while retaining the damaged and dead tree trunks.

If crevices are not available, pine martens may move into buildings. A local politician in our area has pine martens in his house every year and loves them. He always gets my vote. But if they move into your house and you want them to move out again, this must be done with the help of a wildlife ranger. The Vincent Wildlife Trust has a factsheet to help with this issue. It is also wise to stop the martens from getting any food around your house – a special bin-strap has been designed to stop them from raiding your wheelie bin.

Of course, the solution is to provide pine martens with cosy den sites. We recently trialled two types of pine marten box on our farm. One is a large box, developed by the Vincent Wildlife Trust. It has two entrance holes and can be fixed onto a tree. It is fairly heavy, and so can be difficult to put up, so we have also tried a Galloway Lite box, which is a much smaller box inside a plastic tub. As this is lighter, it can be fixed to smaller trees.

How will you know if the box is being used? Pine martens tend to poo on the roof of their boxes if they use them. This is an interesting version of the outdoor loo.

Attracting pine martens to your home

- Save old trees in your area. Even if they are dead, they can be pollarded. This is like a severe haircut, where the branches are removed, but the trunk, with all its cracks and crevices, is left intact. Damaged branches can be propped up with supports.
- Put up some pine marten boxes. Designs are available from the Vincent Wildlife Trust's website *pinemarten.ie*.
- Plant berries of all types. Studies in Britain have found that pine martens love to feast on ivy, blackberries, rowan and bilberries, but any berry will do. So, plant a hedgerow of currants, blackberries and nuts – hazels for example. Both the pine martens and your neighbours will love you for it.
- Put out scraps for the pine marten and use a trail camera to video them. They like to eat berries, fruit, nuts, meat and seeds. They really love jam, but it is probably bad for them to have too much. Our pine marten is very keen on fat balls.

Things to do with pine martens

- Try some pine marten ecotourism. Book a day in a hide in Glory Hides in Laois and go to see a pine marten for yourself. It's a wonderful experience.
- Treat yourself to Johnny Birks' fabulous book *Pine Martens*.

Activities for children

- Become a poo sniffer. Take the children out to a woodland and have a look along branches and fallen logs for poo. You can find pine marten scats at any time of year, but the easiest time to find them is in spring. Studies on pine marten poo showed that there are high cortisol levels (which show stress) in scats that are placed in conspicuous places, compared to scats in more hidden places. Perhaps the process of staking your claim on a territory and marking it is nerve-racking. People find that moving to a new house is pretty stressful. It may be the same for pine martens.

HEDGEHOGS

Several years ago, we were awoken to snorting and grunting sounds. It sounded as if something was about to die just outside the house – perhaps a major disaster had happened to one of our dogs? We rushed out – just in time to find two hedgehogs trundling away. We had accidently broken up a 'first date' that was taking place in our back garden.

In the winter of 2010, the snow descended on our farm in Meath. It blocked roads, with drifts of several feet, and we were snowed in for 6 weeks. And I think it may have killed off the local hedgehogs, as we no longer saw any sign of them. Several years later, having planted hedgerows and set up hibernation sites, we took some hedgehogs from the hedgehog hospital and released them. Neighbours kept us informed on their progress and reported any sightings, and our local school in Maio found tracks in the mud in their playground.

However, numbers still appear to be declining – we rarely find hedgehogs on our trail cameras, in spite of having food out every night. There is a serious decline in hedgehog numbers throughout Europe, and I bet this is happening in Ireland too.

Hedgehogs live throughout Ireland, but dislike wet marshy areas and coniferous woodland. In other countries, they seem to keep away from arable land, perhaps because land with crops is often like a desert – without hedgerows, and with a densely packed monoculture. These fields are often huge to allow large farm machinery to easily manoeuvre around them, and there is nowhere for a hedgehog to feed or nest. But hedgehogs are often found in gardens, and gardeners love them as they eat slugs and snails. Hedgehogs eat beetles too, along with other insects, and have also been known to eat fruit and eggs.

Strangely enough, it is thought that hedgehogs were first brought into Ireland for people to eat. A prickly dish! One of the first records of an Irish hedgehog is from Waterford in the thirteenth century.

A YEAR IN THE LIFE OF A HEDGEHOG

Hedgehogs hibernate for the winter. To do this, they must build up their body weight in the autumn. Hedgehog rehabbers generally say that a hedgehog should be around 600g in weight to have enough fat to survive the winter. A hedgehog weighing less than this can starve over the winter, so if found, they are often taken into care by people and fattened up over the winter.

I have had several hedgehogs on this fattening programme over winter. As the rest of us try to lose weight after Christmas, we try to make the hedgehogs put it on. I feel like the witch in Hansel and Gretel, shoving cat food into hedgehogs that would rather just be left alone to sleep. And they hibernate deeply – their heart rate drops to 20 beats per minute (from 190 beats per minute). They really look dead. I have made this mistake, telling everyone that our hedgehog had died, only to face embarrassment as I realised he was still alive – just in hibernation. It's lucky I don't work in a hospital!

Hedgehogs breed after their first hibernation, and the mother can have two litters a year of 3 to 5 young. Often the second litter will not survive, as the young don't have enough time to build up body fat before hibernation. Pregnancy lasts 5 weeks, and the babies are called piglets. It is very important that the nest is not disturbed, as the mum can abandon the young if frightened. She generally leaves them alone at night while she gets food, and weans them after around 4 weeks. Hedgehogs are solitary animals, and after 6 weeks, the young are keen to go it alone!

Hedgehogs in the wild usually live for around 3 years, with many being killed on the roads between April and July. They love hibernating in areas of fallen branches and logs – be sure to check your bonfire pile for hedgehogs before Halloween!

Attracting hedgehogs to your garden

- Create a hedgehog highway. Talk to your neighbours about leaving small, hedgehog-sized gaps in fences, to allow the animal to move freely from one garden to another. If you want to make the holes in your fence look a little better, you can buy hedgehog designs to put around the holes – so everyone knows what you're doing. This increases the amount of foraging available to the hedgehog.
- Put out small amounts of cat food or dog food. The traditional food we gave hedgehogs was milk and bread, but this is not good for them.
- Stop using slug pellets – hedgehogs may eat the pellets or may eat poisoned slugs. Use copper wire, eggshells, sharp sand or beer traps against slugs instead. When the hedgehogs finally arrive, all your slug problems will be solved.
- Put out drinking water and a pile of logs or a purpose-built hedgehog house.
- If you have a pond, put in a log or a piece of timber that can be used as a hedgehog ramp, allowing hedgehogs and other animals to get out if they fall in.
- Remove any netting, and when out walking, pick up anything hedgehogs could get tangled in. Fruit netting, tennis netting, fishing nets and the plastic rings that hold cans together are lethal. The poor hedgehogs get tangled in them and are stuck.

- Hedgehogs are curious and stick their heads into a range of different pots and jars. So pick up any rubbish you see in the hedgerows or along the roadside. And take part in the An Taisce National Spring Clean!
- Be really, really careful when using a garden strimmer. Many hedgehogs die every year from strimmer injuries.

Activities for children

- Make a paper hedgehog. Fold a paper plate in half and cut spines in it. Colour it in.
- Have a closer look at what hedgehogs eat. Gather some slugs from the garden. Keep them well contained – it is surprising how fast slugs can move and escape! Offer them food and see what happens (I met one slug who really loved red lentils). Then after half an hour or so, release them back to their homes. It's a surprisingly entertaining way to pass a rainy afternoon.

SMALLER MAMMALS

BATS

Our adventures in setting up a bat group began when we invited the eminent scientist Dr Bob Stebbings to Dublin to give us advice. I sounded very professional when I first spoke to him, so he did well to hide his dismay when he was met at the airport by a clueless gang of hairy ecologists (males and females). He squeezed into my small car, with all the gang plus a large bat exhibition.

Worse was to come, as I was just learning to drive – in those days, you were allowed to drive alone before taking a driving test. I had been driving less than one week. With all the excitement – learning to drive, being in awe of the great scientist, and trying to impress the hairy ecologists – I stalled the car midway under the parking barrier at Dublin Airport. I watched in horror as the barrier began to descend on the car, potentially decapitating the learned scientist. (I can tell you now, in case you decide to try this for yourself, that there is some sort of safety mechanism which prevents these barriers from slicing through your roof. It is like a magician's act. The lady doesn't really get sawn in two …)

Bob was either too squashed to notice his potentially impending death, or too kind to mention it, and we continued on our way. He really inspired us and helped us many times over the years in our studies of these fascinating creatures.

There are many types of bat in Ireland. We tend to think of them all as one species: 'the bats'. That's like putting ourselves into a group called 'primates' and giving us all the same food and homes. Although my family might think I act like an orangutan, I definitely have different requirements.

A YEAR IN THE LIFE OF A BAT

Bats hibernate in wintertime. It is difficult to know where they hibernate, as they are so small it is hard to find them, but some hibernate in caves, some in cold buildings and some in trees. Some pick odd places – I found one bat trying to hibernate in a crack in the pavement! But generally, they need a temperature of about 7°C, with enough dampness to prevent their wings from drying out.

Unless you own a Gothic mansion, your house is probably much too warm and dry for bat hibernation. However, if you are lucky enough to own a wine cellar, you might find some trying it out as a natural cave. We attached rows of timber to the roof of our barn, like fake joists, with 18mm gaps between the timbers. This has been highly successful as a bat hibernaculum, with 5 to 7 pipistrelles hibernating in the barn every year. It is a cheap and easy way to make bat hibernation spaces if you happen to have a tall shed.

Bats are not sleeping during hibernation. In fact, one theory on why bats wake in wintertime is for a rest! They might also feel thirsty and awaken for a drink. Sometimes you will see the bats flying in the daytime in winter, having woken from torpor (their hibernation state). If the temperature rises, the bat may also awaken, and go off in search of insects. Bats use up a lot of energy coming out of torpor, so must never be woken up. *Do not disturb!*

In autumn, bats mate. We have noticed that in captivity, male bats get really grumpy in September. Their hormones are at work! Many bats swarm at sites – especially entrances to caves and underground tunnels. It is not really known why they do this, but bat experts spend many hours trapping them and trying to figure it out. Perhaps it is some mating ritual, like something you might see outside your local nightclub.

Having mated in autumn, bats become pregnant in spring. The girls store the sperm over winter and use it when the time is right and there is plenty of food for a pregnant female. Then the females look for somewhere warm to use as a maternity ward. This can be buildings, trees, barns or stonework.

Bat babies are big! The pup is around one-third the size of the mother bat, so bats generally have just a single baby, every one or two years. Generally, the mothers roost together in summer, throwing out males and non-breeding females from the roost. One survey of pipistrelle DNA looked at male bats roosting in bat boxes nearby. The ones closest to the maternity roost were likely to have fathered more pups. So clearly the females don't want to travel too far for romance.

Sometimes bats set up a harem in a bat box, where males group in twos and threes, calling to the females. There doesn't seem to be any competition between them, and the female enters the box for romance. Again, we don't know what happens next – whether she chooses one or shares all three.

Bats eat insects – lots of them. Pipistrelles can eat up to 3,000 insects per night! Some bats chase their prey, and some creep up silently on moths and munch them. If you have ever driven at night and noticed moths falling to the ground in front of your car, it is because they think your car is a bat and have evolved to drop suddenly out of the sky to avoid being eaten. One theory holds that the furriness of moths is to confuse the echolocation of bats – they get a blurry image that might just give the moth the chance to escape.

Bats have to put on a lot of body weight in order to make it through the winter, so you will see them feeding furiously in September, while shouting at each other. They are very social animals, and we often record male social calls when out doing surveys.

And then to hibernation. Most bats have finished mating by winter, but some male bats are opportunists and will sneak up on a female while she is hibernating. I have seen photos of Daubenton's females, hibernating in a cave with defrosted bottoms! They will wake up with a surprise pregnancy.

ECHOLOCATION

'As blind as a bat' turns out to be a lie. Bats can see, and many species have noticeably big eyes. However, as we all know, it is difficult to see in the dark, so bats have developed an ultrasound system to catch their food. It is quite remarkable. I worked for many years in a hospital in an ultrasound department, and the machines I used cost in excess of €500,000. Yet these machines can't see with the level of detail that bats can. Bats use ultrasound to navigate, find food and communicate with each other.

So, what exactly is ultrasound? Sound travels in waves, and the higher the number of waves passing a point, the higher the pitch. Give it a try (unless you are on the bus). If you sing a high note, you are making a high-frequency sound. Sing a low note, and you have a low frequency. Our hearing works in the range from 20Hz to 20kHz (20 to 20,000 waves per second). Generally, we can't hear above 20kHz, although some children can, and the top range of our hearing decreases as we get older.

Some animals sing so low that we can't hear them at all – their frequency is below 20Hz. Next time you visit a zoo and see the giraffe throwing back his head, he may be speaking to you. But he is using a low-frequency sound (infrasound), and you can't hear him. Bats use the other end of the scale. Generally speaking, the bigger you are, the lower your pitch – elephants make low-frequency sounds, while bats make high-frequency sounds. And in our batty world, bigger bats (like Leisler's) use lower-frequency sounds, while smaller bats (like pipistrelles) use higher pitches. This doesn't always follow exactly, but it's a good rule of thumb when identifying bats.

High-frequency sounds allow the bat to see in detail, but the sounds don't travel very far. It is a little like putting reading glasses on – you can read the newspaper very well, but you can't see far away. Lower-frequency signals allow the bat to look further into the distance, but are not as good for small objects. This impacts upon bats' feeding styles. Bats with high-frequency signals can catch really tiny insects (midges, for example), but get a little lost in wide open spaces. Bats such as the Leisler's bat can fly around easily in open fields with their lower-frequency ultrasound, but must catch bigger insects.

Of course, this is a simplistic view, as most bats move through a range of frequencies, just as we change the focus of our eyes to look at the bus or text a friend. However, it gives an idea of how different bat species operate differently.

How often do bats call? This seems to be tied in with their wing flapping. In order to get a good loud shout while flying, bats pull in a good lungful of air as they open their wings. You can try this at home too. Putting your arms out and shoulders back expands your ribcage, letting air in – it's a technique used by people when public speaking. For a bat, flapping your wings in flight must help push out air, meaning that it takes less energy to shout. Some species (such as Daubenton's bats) have a steady flap and a regular ultrasound signal, while others, such as whiskered bats, have an irregular shout and are very flappy in flight.

It takes a lot of energy to shout. A study on Nathusius' pipistrelles in Germany showed that when competing with human-made ultrasonic noise, the bats had to shout at 128 decibels. The researchers said that the bats normally shout at about the volume level of a chainsaw, but when the human-generated ultrasonic noise appeared, they had to increase their volume to that of a jet engine. This increase in volume used a lot of energy. To create this energy, they would have to eat an extra 7% of their body weight every night. I am 65kg, so if I were a bat, I would have to eat an extra 4.5kg of food every day just to shout above human ultrasonic noise. That is an astonishing amount extra needed on top of your daily rations. In many public areas, ultrasound devices are placed to discourage teenagers from gathering. These 'teen tormenter' devices can only be heard by young people. For the sake of teenagers, as well as bats, these devices should be switched off.

Bats can live for twenty years. This is extraordinarily long for a mammal of that size! As with all wild animals, the death rate in the first year is high, but if they survive that, the pipistrelle often lives for five years, and has been found living up to sixteen years.

One rule of thumb says that most lifespans last a billion heartbeats. (Before you panic, humans get 2 to 3 billion heartbeats, and also have modern medicine.) So small animals with high heart rates live short, fast lives, and die young. For example, a hamster has around 450 heartbeats per minute and lives around 3 years, while an elephant with 70 heartbeats per minute lives around 70 years.

But this doesn't seem to apply to bats, who must raise their heartrate to fly and echolocate. Some interesting work is being carried out by Professor Emma Teeling in University College Dublin on bats and aging. In addition to living longer than normal, bats do not seem to suffer from problems relating to aging, such as arthritis.

Dr Teeling is looking at bats' DNA – specifically, she is investigating their telomeres – caps at the ends of our chromosomes, which prevent them from deteriorating or fusing with other chromosomes. Telomeres act like the bits of plastic on our shoelaces, preventing our shoelaces (or genes) from fraying. As we get older, our telomeres get shorter. However, the telomere length on bats doesn't appear to change with age. Do bats hold the secret to eternal youth?

BAT DETECTORS

Treat yourself! Buy a bat detector. Very basic kits can be purchased to make your own detector for under €40. And for under €100 you can have a tuneable, basic bat detector that allows you to hear batty sounds. Bat detectors move the bat ultrasound down to frequencies that can be heard by the human ear. Tuning the detector to 45kHz will give you the common pipistrelle, 25kHz will give you Leisler's bats and 55kHz will give you soprano pipistrelles. You will soon get used to the sounds of the different species. Myotis bats can be difficult to tell apart on these heterodyne detectors (detectors that combine 2 frequencies to create one that we can hear), but they are difficult to tell apart anyway!

If you want to spend more cash, you can purchase a time-expansion bat detector. This allows you to download ultrasound files to your computer and use a software package to identify the species. Some of these detectors allow you to see a screen so you can look at the signals while the bats are flying about. This is especially useful if you have a quiet and a loud species flying around together. With a heterodyne detector, you will only hear the loud bat, so you will assume both bats are the same species. A time-expansion detector records all signals, so it is really great when you have a few bats flying together. You can also spend many happy hours looking at bat signals and making measurements on your computer.

Time expansion detectors and their analysis packages are very expensive. Like a musical instrument, you come to love your own detector, and know its own quirky ways. Mine might just be the first possession I would save if my house was burning down.

Bats' eyes are used to working in darkness. Turn on a spotlight and they can be dazzled. Bright lights create a physical barrier to bats and can stop them getting to their roosting places. In addition, moths are drawn to the lighting, and flap in circles until they are exhausted.

The dark spaces become like deserts, with all food sucked away by lighting, leaving the bats to starve. Some bats try to chase after insects under lighting. But they are at risk of being eaten by predators – now birds and cats can easily see them, as they no longer have the protection of the night.

So, turn off all outdoor lights! At a minimum, keep lighting low, with the use of bollard or ground lights – so people can see pathways and tracks, but the light does not spill up into the trees and sky. There should never be lighting on waterways. Waterways are the bat motorway system, where they commute, feed and drink. Bridges should never be floodlit.

It is important to check if bats are using old buildings like churches before putting lights on them. Small 'fairy light'-type lights can be used to highlight a pretty feature of a building without floodlighting an entire building.

Artificial lighting also causes problems for human health, disrupting the production of melatonin.

So, SWITCH IT OFF!

BAT BOXES

If you had a choice of where to live, would you choose a cool, draughty box or a large, warm space? You know the answer –

and bats feel the same way about it. The best bat box you can give is your attic. Failing that, the fascia board around your house is often very popular. If you have a hot chimney area or a boiler, bats will love it.

Bat boxes are the student accommodation of the bat world. Usually inhabited by a couple of single males or non-breeding females, they act as temporary living places. Think of the TV show 'Friends'. At some stage, they will want somewhere bigger and better to rear their pups. But as a bachelor pad, a bat box is great. Some species suit bat boxes better than others, but if you put up a few boxes, it is likely they will be used.

The most important thing about the boxes is that the entrance gap into them must be small. There is a wonderful animal behaviourist called Temple Grandin. She is on the autistic spectrum and feels that this helps her understand animals better. She says that when she was young and over-whelmed, she would lie under the cushions of the family sofa and ask the family to sit on it. The feeling of being squashed made her feel secure. Her work shows that many animals like being squashed – for example, animals such as cats and cattle. When you think of it, it is the reason we all like a hug. I think bats also like to be squashed. If the entrance gap of a bat box is too wide, bats will not use it – they just don't feel safe.

The ideal gap is about 15–18mm for Irish bats – about the size of your thumb. Bat boxes bought from abroad often have wider gaps, which are suitable for their bigger species, but make our bats feel unsafe. It's a little like having a lovely house with no front door.

Research in Poland has looked at Leisler's bats and their roosts in trees. Pine martens are happy to snack on Leisler's bats, so the researchers looked at how the bats avoid being eaten during hibernation. Firstly, the bats choose really high crevices, which are more difficult for the marten to climb to. Then they choose a narrow entrance hole. And finally, they choose a deep crevice – deeper than the arm's length of a pine marten, which may be swiping aimlessly at them. It's like trying to catch a furry toy with a claw machine at a funfair.

In May, the pregnant mums-to-be search out a maternity ward in which to have their young. Pregnant bats are fussy about their living spaces. They need a really warm place in which to rear their pups, with a temperature of about 30°C. This is so hot, I really couldn't believe it, until I bought myself a thermometer and started measuring the heat in roosts.

Bats have one pup every year or two. This is why the populations of bats are so fragile – the numbers of babies born per bat are low, and as with all wild animals, many young bats die within the first year. It also means that the numbers of bats in your house won't change much from year to year. If the numbers change, it means there has been a local catastrophe.

We usually have ten to twenty common pipistrelles in our attic over the summer months. One year, the number went up to eighty bats. One of our neighbours was re-roofing their house, and their bats must have come to us. Since then, we have only a few bats each year. Clearly the re-roofing was a great success, and their attic is now much cosier than ours!

BATS IN HOUSES

If you have bats in your attic, you are a hero. You are providing a real nature reserve and doing enormous work for bat conservation.

Bats will not damage the fabric of your house. They have tiny teeth, so they cannot chew up your wiring. This unfortunately acts against them, as new breathable fabrics are used within newer buildings. With time, these fabrics wear down and threads are exposed. The threads wrap around bats' legs and trap them. Because the threads are of hard plastic, the bats are unable to chew them, and they die entangled. Some horrible cases have been recorded of whole roosts dying in Britain. So, if you are re-roofing your house and you want bats, use old-fashioned bituminous felt under the slates.

Another issue with roofing is timber treatment. Bats are particularly susceptible to poisoning with timber treatments, as they often lie directly against rafters. It's bad for the bats, but there are also cases of children being poisoned by the timber treatments of their bedroom rafters and playground equipment. Thankfully, safer products are being developed, but timber treatments should only be used when absolutely necessary.

There are a variety of bat slates available, which you can fix to your roof. These have a small gap built into the slate, allowing bats to access the attic. I find that bats love entering roofs under ridge tiles at the ends of a house, and cement can easily be removed in these places to create a small gap for bats to crawl in.

If you are building a new house, a bat brick can be put in place. This has an open, letterbox-like gap, and is built into the wall at a height above 3 metres. You can have fun telling small children that your postman is very tall, and you built it especially for him! We have one of these and pipistrelles and brown long eared bats have used it (but no postman!).

It is important to cover water tanks in attics, as bats can drown in them. Other than that, you should have no problems with bats in the attic. In cases of large roosts, usually of soprano pipistrelles, the droppings can build up and smell can become a problem. A layer of plastic on the floor of your attic will catch the droppings and can be removed each year – and often a local bat group or wildlife ranger will help with this. If smell is an issue, zeolite can be used to mop up the smell. Another convenient smell collector is cat litter! Place some in trays around the attic and the smell should vanish. However, the build-up of smells is rare and really only happens with large roosts in unventilated spaces.

Bats generally make very little noise in an attic, though sometimes children can hear their ultrasound. My children can hear them, and it's reassuring for them to have their little pet bats living above their bedrooms. As we get older, our hearing range lowers, and as adults we can't hear bats.

If you have bats in your attic, count them in early May (before they have bred), and in August (when the babies are flying), to see how many babies your maternity ward has delivered. The babies start flying in late July and early August. They must learn to fly, echolocate and catch insects all at once.

It's not surprising that many make mistakes at this stage. Like all adolescents, they tend to go wandering, exploring the great outside world, and can accidently wander into your house, or miss the entrance to the attic and come in through your bedroom window. Don't panic – remember, this is a lost baby. Keep your windows closed at dusk and dawn in late July/August, or pin a net curtain around the window. The bats will see this and will not fly in.

If a bat has flown into your bedroom and has now disappeared, have a look for it in the folds of your curtains. Remember that bats like to be squashed and will feel safe crammed into your curtain folds. Pick it up using a towel or a pot, sliding cardboard under it (the way we used to catch bees as children!). Then put the bat on an upstairs window ledge or a high point outside at dusk. Bats need to drop to take off easily, so they should be able to drop from your window ledge. A high window ledge is also safe from cats. Check on it in the morning and call a vet or wildlife ranger if it's still there. Hopefully, it will have flown away by itself or been collected by its mum.

Identifying bats
- There are several ways we identify bats:
- What colour is it?
- What size is it?
- Does it have a post-calcarial lobe, and what shape is it? The calcar is a piece of cartilage running from the bat's leg to the wing, and some bats have a lobe (an extra bit of skin) hanging from this cartilage.
- What does its tragus look like? A tragus is a small lump in front of the ear canal. In some species it is small and round; in others it is long and pointed.

THE PIPISTRELLES

When I was first learning about bats, we thought that all pipistrelles were the same. They act in similar ways, and they look similar. Examination of their DNA has revealed that there are three different species of pipistrelle in Ireland.

COMMON PIPISTRELLES

This tiny bat lives throughout Irel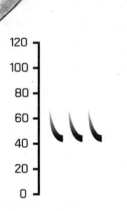 but is less common in the west. I lives in a range of habitats, and is often found in houses in summertime, where small maternity roosts are formed, usually of under 30 bats.

The common pipistrelle echolocates at a peak frequency of 45kHz, so is easy to identify on a bat detector. The signal looks 'L'-shaped.

This bat is often called a bandit, because it has a black face – it looks as if it is wearing a mask. If you see one up close, its tragus is usually rounded, broad and brown. My husband swears that he can tell common and soprano pipistrelles apart by smelling them, but I'm not sure that is a recognised identification method.

It's a lovely little bat. We had Pippa the rescued bat living with us for a while. She had been in a battle with a cat and came off the worst. Unfortunately, her wing was broken, and never healed, but she would come out and sit on your hand when her cage was opened. Sadly, she died of her injuries.

SOPRANO PIPISTRELLES

When people have problems with bats in their attic, it is usually this species. This little bat also likes to have its young inside houses, but lives in a bigger gang of girls. As anyone who has lived with me knows, a gang of girls together can get noisy and messy. But these bats are great, so please do your best to tolerate them!

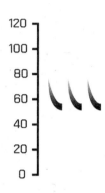

They have a pinkish face and a rounded, broad tragus. They also have a lumpier nose than the common pipistrelle, as they have more glands in their nose. Each bat eats up to 3,000 insects per night.

Soprano pipistrelles echolocate at 55kHz, with an 'L'-shaped signal, and you will hear them all over Ireland. You will often see them in pairs, shouting and chasing each other. I would love to know what they are saying.

NATHUSIUS' PIPISTRELLES

I don't know how we ever managed to mix this bat up with the other two pipistrelles. Nathusius' pipistrelles are hairy, tough and extremely brave, the muscle men and women of the tiny bat world. I went to visit a roost in Northern Ireland. The weather was terrible – cold, wild, windy and wet – and I was about to give up, as bats (just like people) hate this type

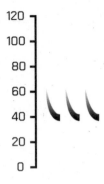

of weather. Then over Lough Neagh – a huge, choppy lake – came these tiny bats, battling the elements. I was astonished.

It is thought that these bats migrate long distances throughout Europe. A friend of mine was trapping and ringing birds in northern France, and a Nathusius' pipistrelle flew into his net. He carefully untangled and released it and noticed that it had a ring on its leg. When he traced the ring number, he found that its ring had been placed on it in Lithuania. What a distance to travel! Perhaps some even migrate to and from Ireland.

There are problems with ringing bats. Birds have defined legs, so rings can easily be put on them, but bats have delicate skin that attaches just above the leg, and both leg and membrane can be damaged by rings. That is why bat ringing is only undertaken rarely, and under strict scientific and legal conditions. New rings, which are smoother and more polished, are being developed, but it is still a delicate procedure.

There is one very odd thing about the Nathusius' pipistrelle – the females don't like the Republic of Ireland. Although there are several maternity roosts recorded in Northern Ireland, there has only been one maternity roost recorded in southern Ireland – in Wexford. We find male roosts throughout Ireland, and in fact one male Nathusius' pipistrelle calls hopefully in my back garden in summertime. But he is out of luck. The females won't cross the border, and we don't know why.

The tragus of the Nathusius' pipistrelle is curved and slightly rounded. On a bat detector, their ultrasound signal has an

'L'-shape, and the bottom of the 'L' is at 39kHz. It is easy to confuse with a common pipistrelle with a low voice. But if you are in the Republic of Ireland, and you record a Nathusius' pipistrelle, it is probably a male!

THE *MYOTIS* SPECIES

If you want to get rich quick, run a course called 'How to tell the *Myotis* species apart'. I take several courses of this type every year, but the problem is that *Myotis* bats are really difficult to identify on a detector. Your chances of telling them apart are increased if you manage to catch sight of them. I recommend the excellent book *British Bat Calls: A guide to species identification* by Dr Jon Russ for further reading. However, I will attempt to give you a brief overview of the mysterious *Myotis*.

DAUBENTON'S BATS

This bat is really easy to identify, as it generally flies above water in horizontal lines, about one metre from the surface. It likes still rather than choppy water and eats the insects flying just above water level. If you visit any pond or canal in summer and hang around long enough, you will see one. Surprisingly, it is difficult to see them if you are looking down over them. The best way is to get low along the bank so that you are level with their flight.

You might get strange looks from people passing, but you can pretend that you are doing some night-time paddling.

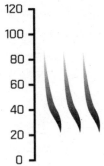

Daubenton's bats have really big feet and a slight bald area around their eyes, which makes them look as if they are wearing glasses. The bats under a year old often have a brown mark on their mouths, which seems to vanish as they get older.

Daubenton's bats live in stonework in bridges and old buildings. They are extremely sensitive to lighting. We monitor Daubenton's bats along our local River Borora in Meath every year. Unfortunately, a local group installed very pretty lighting on the bridge along the river. The light shone onto the river and all the bats suddenly vanished. We were able to show the data to the group and they were delighted to help the bats. They painted the side of the lanterns black, so no light falls onto the river, while light still shines along the roadway. The bats are now returning, the bridge looks pretty, the water is dark, and everyone is happy!

Daubenton's bats have a loud ultrasound, with a very regular beat. On the bat detector, it sweeps from around 85kHz to 25kHz and looks like a vertical line, with a small lump or bend in it around 40kHz.

WHISKERED BATS

This bat is uncommon and difficult to find in Ireland. It can sometimes be seen within forests, along tracks or near rivers. It has shaggy hair and a grey belly and flutters its wings a lot when it flies.

We don't know of many roosts in Ireland, and I would be ecstatic if I found one, but whiskered bats can use old buildings to roost in.

When is a whiskered not a whiskered? When it's a Brandt's! The Brandt's bat looks almost exactly like the whiskered bat. There is a slight difference in their teeth and the shape of their penis, but examining them would amount to sexual abuse of bats, so I wouldn't recommend it. The only definite way to tell them apart is by DNA analysis. We have one record of a Brandt's bat in Wicklow, but it is possible that there are more out there, disguised as whiskered bats.

Imagine you are lying in bed with your children when a giant monster suddenly walks in. What would you do? You would probably get hysterical. Whiskered bats are notorious for getting hysterical when you enter a roost, screaming and shouting little batty curses at you. And who could blame them?

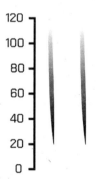

The ultrasound of whiskered bats is irregular, moving from around 85kHz down to 30kHz in a single line – an 'I'-shape.

NATTERER'S BATS

I first found a roost of Natterer's bats in a bridge in Galway twenty years ago, and I have been hooked on them ever since. They can really zip around the air and have a zig-zag flight with sharp turns – now you see them, now you don't! Close up, they have bristly hairs on their tail membrane. This might help them when catching insects. I've watched young bats practising their skills flicking food into their tail membranes. It must be like football practice! Natterer's bats have a 'S'-shaped calcar (the piece of cartilage running from their ankle to their wing membrane).

I have found Natterer's bats living in farm buildings, and they love to roost in underground tunnels in wintertime. They tend to like the tall, square towers found on Protestant churches in Ireland. They are often found swarming in groups in Britain around the entrances of caves in autumn. It is assumed that this is some kind of mating ritual – the bat version of a disco or rave.

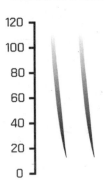

The echolocation of Natterer's bats looks like a long vertical line – an 'l'-shape. It can start extremely high and move incredibly low – from over 100kHz down to 20kHz, with an irregular pulse. Imagine a mad drummer, hitting all sorts of pitches and rhythms while moving in odd directions across the sky.

OTHER IRISH BATS

BROWN LONG-EARED BATS

If the Natterer's bat is the Protestant bat, this is the Catholic bat. It really loves big attics and the type of high roof that you find in Catholic churches. It also loves to live in the large attics of mansions (who wouldn't?), but if that isn't available, it will roost in stonework in farm buildings. I have one living outside in a small garden shed. Presumably, it lives in hope that one day I'll win the lottery and build it a large mansion. Or church.

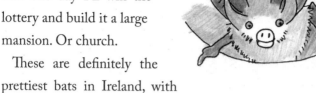

These are definitely the prettiest bats in Ireland, with large, long, rabbit-like ears. Perhaps you can wiggle your ears, but the long-eared bat has perfected this and can move each ear independently backwards and forwards. It is a wonderful trick skill to have when listening to rustling and sneaking up on an unsuspecting moth.

When eating moths and butterflies, brown long-eared bats spit out the bits that taste nasty. Clearly the wings of these insects taste disgusting – as the bat finishes up its dinner, it spits a little pile of wings on the floor. This is an easy way to find long-eared bats – just search an old building for dinner leftovers on the floor. A small stack of wings is a giveaway.

Brown long-eared bats are very conservative. Females like to shop locally, rarely travelling more than 1.5km from home. Males might go a little further, but this species is very home-loving. They like to have a roost close to food and water – why would you leave? They're also very suspicious of anything new – one study showed that it took 4 years before a long-eared bat investigated a new bat box. Perhaps the secret of their success is that they are a cautious, conservative bat that knows what it likes. Surprisingly, their small roosts, which don't travel, are not inbred. How this happens remains a mystery to be solved.

You can easily be fooled by a long-eared bat when you are looking at it tucked into a crevice. It can pull its long ears right back, so all you can see is the tragus. The tragus of a brown long-eared bat is big and looks like the ear of a Natterer's bat. So you imagine that you are seeing a Natterer's bat that is somehow missing its own tragus. Just one of the many ways bats can confuse us!

If you see a bat and you can't see anything on your bat detector, it is probably a long-eared bat. They are *really* quiet. Their top frequency is around 55kHz, dropping down to about 25kHz, and it looks like one 'I'-shape overlapping another 'I'-shape on a time-expansion detector.

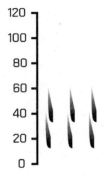

If you enter a roost after dusk and see lots of bats just flying about inside a building, you could be watching long-eared bats light-sampling. The bats whizz around inside the roost, looking out the entrance now and again to see if it's time to go out. I suppose it's like getting ready to go to a party. I have seen some long-eared bats take advantage of insects mesmerised by Velux windows. The bats fly up to the window and have a quick insect snack before leaving. When they decide that it is dark enough, they head outside.

LEISLER'S BATS

The Leisler's bat is our biggest, furriest and loudest bat. I often think a male Leisler's bat has a mane – a shaggy piece of fur across its shoulders. A friend had an injured Leisler's bat for many years, and it loved a massage across its shoulders with a paintbrush.

The Leisler's bat is strong. It can fly high in the air and, because of its size, can eat bigger insects such as dung beetles. It has a rounded, lumpy tragus (in its rounded, lumpy ear). Leisler's bats are found in small numbers throughout Europe, but in high numbers in Ireland, so Ireland is especially important for this species. Bat workers come from abroad just to record this bat, and it happily turns up everywhere for them.

In summertime, it often roosts in houses and has also been found roosting in trees. We frequently find male Leisler's bats setting up mating perches in trees in autumn. It can also fly in the open, and you will see it over fields and parks.

It has a deep, loud voice, and you will find it on your bat detector around 25kHz, with an 'L'-shape.

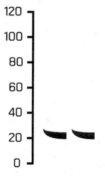

LESSER HORSESHOE BATS

If you come across one of these, it's time to get really excited! There are between 12,000 and 14,000 of these bats left in Ireland. Throughout Europe, they are very rare, and the population in Ireland is crucially important.

The bat gets its name from its strange horseshoe-shaped nose, which it shouts through to echolocate. It loves to hang freely, like the bats you see hanging about in horror films – most of our other bats tuck themselves away during the daytime. And it is very, very fussy about where it lives.

In summertime, the females like to live in large attics, preferably of giant castles or ruins, or failing that, the ruins of farm buildings. In winter, they like to live in caves or underground cellars.

You can see why this obsession with ruined buildings can lead to problems for the bats. Ruined buildings tend to fall down eventually. And people with large castles and wine cellars may not want to share them with bats. In fairness, both the super-rich and bats tend to suffer from bad public relations. And yet I have met several people living in fabulous castles and houses who tolerate these bats living with them, and even go to great lengths to protect them.

One man went to even greater lengths than most. Twenty years ago, I wrote to everyone I could think of, asking if they could help us protect bats. And I came across an amazing man. Vincent Weir was a multi-millionaire shipping magnate, who decided to use his fortune to save one species. And the species he chose was the lesser horseshoe bat. Of course, I wrote to him, speaking of the problems of bats in their collapsing buildings. And like Santa Claus, he delivered! Within 24 hours, he was working on organising staff and protecting roosts. He paid farmers to put roofs on collapsing farm buildings. And when the collapse had gone too far, he built buildings especially for the horseshoe bat.

And it worked. Numbers of this species began to increase. Sadly, Vincent Weir died in 2014. Bat workers throughout the world (including myself) shed tears. He left his fortune to wildlife conservation, and the amazing work of the Vincent Wildlife Trust continues!

Irish organisations also became involved, with the Heritage Council buying the largest summer roost of lesser horseshoes in Ireland, in County Clare.

These bats have very exacting requirements for roosting. They like to fly directly into a roost (whereas other bats will land and crawl in), so roosts must have a good opening – a window gap on a derelict building is perfect. Crucially, they need underground areas to hibernate in. That is why they are only found in the west of Ireland, where underground caves are found in limestone areas.

Another issue is with their ultrasound. Lesser horseshoe bats have a short ultrasound wavelength. This effectively makes them 'short-sighted'. Being short-sighted myself, I can understand what this is like. They don't like open spaces, instead flying along hedgerows or treelines – basically they 'feel' their way along, using hedgerows as navigational aids. So, they need hedgerows without gaps, leading from their roosts to their feeding areas. What happens when they meet a road? They fly low, close to the road, using the road as their pathway, and they end up getting killed. A green bridge has been built over the M17 Galway–Sligo road, which allows the bats to pass safely between their roost in Kiltartan Cave and their feeding grounds in Coole Park.

But there is another problem. These bats live in two main groups, one in the Clare/Galway area and the other in the Cork/Kerry area. Both these areas have great hedgerows, castles and collapsing buildings, but there is a gap in the Limerick area. The buildings they used to mate in have collapsed, so the populations in Galway and the populations in

Kerry are becoming increasingly inbred. So how do we get bats to meet (and mate) in Limerick?

Luckily, the Vincent Wildlife Trust has a plan. They hope to build little huts (which look like pump houses) throughout farms in Limerick. They have plotted good hedgerow connectivity along the routes. Basically, if you are a female bat from Clare, you will have a good road network taking you to the local disco, where you might meet a Kerryman. The farmers with great hedges connecting one side of Limerick to another are delighted to put these sheds in place. Ideally, they would also be trained to carry out roost monitoring. The problem with this '*Tinder* for bats' scheme is the cost – it is expensive to save a species.

These bats love to glean their food by sneaking up on insects in hedges and along hazel scrub. However, mature hedgerows, hazel scrub and other wildlife features such as ponds are classed as 'unproductive' land by the Department of Agriculture, and farmers are penalised by losing grants for having them. As a result, many of these features are ripped out, and the horseshoe's local restaurant is closed.

You won't mistake the calls of a lesser horseshoe bat. It is the only Irish bat that calls at a frequency of around 111kHz. It can give a flat signal or an 'n'-shaped signal. So, twirl the dial up on your bat detector, go and visit the west of Ireland, and see what you can find.

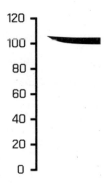

BATS AND TREES

Bats have different preferences for trees, depending on their species. In general, bats with long, narrow wings fly quickly without rapid twists and turns, while those with wider wings can move around more easily and even hover in a clutter of branches. Because of this, we need to have a range of different tree types – what is called a mosaic of woodland types.

The single large tree in the field is wonderful. We have some single oaks in our fields. They look amazing and provide shelter for grazing animals. And our Leisler's bat loves them, happily flying over open pastures with his big wings to munch on insects around the oak tree.

Common pipistrelles have narrower wings and enjoy vertical variation in trees – they love to zip up and down at amazing speed, raising themselves high into the canopy and sky, then falling lower to smaller trees and bushes. They may just be showing off.

But in general, most bats like forest edges, tracks and paths, where they can move easily and gather up insects. Old and damaged trees provide gaps, cracks and crevices, and even dead trees can have fantastic hollows and should be left to stand and decay naturally.

Bats also need height. Size matters where tree roosts are involved! Hedgerows should be allowed to grow tall, and a range of different types of hedgerow should be planted. One size does not fit all, so variety is the key to attracting different species of wildlife. Trees and hedgerows are roadways for wildlife, so when planting a hedge, have a look at Google Maps and see where it can connect to another hedge, another forest, or a pond or waterway. There is little point in building a motorway if it leads nowhere!

I used to be a purist, planting only native trees on my farm. However, having seen bats and other species using imported trees, I have changed my approach. We also had a problem with a disease called ash dieback – as I speak, 10,000 ash trees that I planted in our forest are infected with the disease and may be slowly dying. So, although I plant mostly native trees, I have a few non-native trees planted as a backup in case of emergencies. This year, I planted a few giant American red-woods. They will grow to be enormous, with deep crevices in their bark. I have seen brown long-eared bats tucked away in such folds. And the horse chestnut trees on our farm provide a bumper crop of pollinating insects as food when they come into flower. The whole tree comes alive with buzzing and the bats hoover up the insects. It's like shopping in Dublin city on Christmas Eve.

Attracting bats to hedges and forest

- Plant lots of different types of trees and hedging. Native is best, but feel free to add a few exotic species too.
- Ensure that there are a range of tree heights (roughness) and woodland edge species types. This will allow bats to move up and down easily and provide a variety of insect types.
- Protect and retain old and dead trees. They are the most important trees in the forest.
- Adding a few single trees to grassland and pasture greatly improves its nature value.
- Connect hedges to other hedges.

- Create lots of woodland edges, paths, tracks and gaps. Bats love to feed in these areas.

Batty things to do

- Take part in Bat Conservation Ireland's Daubenton's monitoring programme. They will supply you with a bat detector and training, and you will be asked to walk along a stretch of waterway twice in August and count the numbers of bats passing. We have been surveying our local waterway for fifteen years now, and it's really interesting to see the change over the years.
- Buy a bat detector – or even better, make your own. Unbelievably cheap bat detectors and bat detector kits can be purchased online. They might not be sensitive enough to differentiate species, but they are an invaluable aid to bat watching – it can be really difficult to see bats without the aid of a detector. Then go to a place where there might be bats – often a local river is best. Bats should come out in summertime after sunset.
- Build and put up bat boxes – this is a great activity to do with the community. I've been bat box building for many years, and it's always great fun to do in a group. Bat box kits are readily available. Just remember to keep the entrance gap narrow – around 18mm, or the bats won't use them!
- Switch off all outdoor lights.
- *A word of warning: All bats and their roosts are protected by law, so never disturb, handle or photograph a bat without a licence from the NPWS.*

Activities for children

- If you know of a roost, have a summer sleepover party, and get the children up one hour before dawn. You should be treated to a spectacular display of swarming, where bats circle and twirl before going into their roost. It is wonderful to see.
- Go on a bat walk. Bat Conservation Ireland provide lots of walks and talks during Biodiversity Week and Heritage Week. Children love the excitement of a night-time walk with a torch, watching a Daubenton's bat over a pond.

SHREWS
PYGMY SHREWS

Shrews live life in the fast lane. They are constantly on the move, eating and running around. They are like the lads from the Happy Pear Café – you will never fail to be amazed at their high energy levels.

To maintain these energy levels, pygmy shrews need to eat all the time – they can starve if they go without food for as little as two hours. Like small children, they constantly eat whatever is available. Pygmy shrews particularly like woodlice, beetles and spiders. They are a small mammal, with brown fur and an exceptionally long nose. Their eyesight is poor, so they wiggle their whiskers, using touch and smell to find their food.

I have iron filings in my teeth from many years of visits to the dentist, but my teeth are nothing in comparison to the pygmy shrew. They have natural iron deposits in their teeth, which makes their teeth stronger. This is important when you are a tiny mammal and even an earthworm is too big to tackle. It is thought that the iron deposits also protects the enamel of the teeth against acid. In addition, it adds an amazing reddish tinge to the tooth colour.

If you have a cat, it may have brought you back a pygmy shrew. Shrews must taste and smell disgusting, because cats and foxes often catch shrews, but then refuse to eat them. Because of this, you can sometimes find little shrew bodies lying around.

A YEAR IN THE LIFE OF A PYGMY SHREW

Shrews live in grasslands, hedgerows and forests. They are too weak to burrow, but often live in abandoned mouse burrows, under logs or in stone walls. Long grass is important to them, as it provides food (insects) and a place to hide from predators.

Shrews tend to live alone, and studies have found up to 25 shrews living separately in one hectare. They breed between April and October, and after a pregnancy of 22 to 25 days, the mum has a litter of 4 to 6 young. She can have up to three litters per year, often in a nest of grass. The pygmy shrew can make surprisingly loud squeaks for such a small animal. The squeak is remarkably high-pitched, but children can clearly hear them. The frequency range of our hearing drops as we get older, so we may not hear shrews as adults. So, listen to your children if they tell you that the grass is squeaking. They're not imagining it – they're listening to secret messages from the pygmy shrews.

Pygmy shrews have to eat at least their own bodyweight in insects every day. No wonder they lead such busy lives! Gardeners love them, as they can eat small snails. For our smallest mammal, they have a wild heart, with up to 1,000 heartbeats per minute. Even with double espressos on board, we could never achieve the energy levels of the pygmy shrew.

GREATER WHITE-TOOTHED SHREWS

The pygmy shrew had the island of Ireland to itself until 2007, when people began to notice odd skeletal remains in barn owl and kestrel pellets. What was this? Had pygmy shrews suddenly become bigger?

Analysis of the bones showed that they had found a new species, the greater white-toothed shrew. As the name suggests, the shrew's teeth are white, lacking the iron that gives the reddish tinge to the pygmy shrew's teeth. They don't need reinforced teeth, as they are a bigger and stronger animal. In Italy, research on their diet shows that they mostly eat insects, and can happily eat insects which are 1cm long, though they prefer bite-sized insect snacks of around 3mm.

The greater white-toothed shrew is greyish-brown, with white hairs on its tail. It was first found in Tipperary in 2007, but is thought to have been here since 2001. It is now spreading throughout the country. I found one myself while cycling on the Mullingar Greenway. It must also taste nasty, as it is common enough to find little dead bodies that predators have decided not to eat.

Strangely, every dead shrew I have found has had a horrible grimace on its face, snarling and showing its teeth. It makes them easy to identify, and let's face it, none of us look at our best when dead. Perhaps it was its last attempt to fight off its opponent.

The pygmy shrew is thought to have come to Ireland from Andorra, in the eastern Pyrenees, 8000 years ago. But how did this new animal arrive in Ireland 20 years back? Scientists examining the jaws of the greater white-toothed shrew think that the jaws are similar to jaws found in France, Belgium and Switzerland. DNA analysis seems to place the origins of this new species as France.

Anyone who watches rugby gets anxious when some large, strong Frenchmen takes to the field. But will these new French guys take over from our pygmy shrew? This is a serious concern, as these stronger shrews may tend to take over food and habitat currently occupied by pygmy shrews and wood mice. This could have a serious effect on the pygmy shrew and even the wood mouse population.

But it's not all bad news. Barn owls and kestrels don't have the same taste preferences as foxes and will happily eat these bigger shrews. And a bigger shrew means a bigger snack. Because shrews eat insects, they have no interest in eating poisoned grain (or any grain!). This means that the shrew will not be poisoned and will not pass this poison on to the owl when the owl eats it. It is thought that the presence of this new mammal might help the spread of the barn owl.

Attracting shrews to your area

- Let grass grow long, and sow flowers and plants that attract insects.

- Provide shelter in the form of piles of stones, a stone wall (with gaps in it) or a log pile.

Activities for children

- Shrews have been recorded as having up to 12 body movements per second. Get the children off the sofa and see how many body movements they can do in 15 seconds.

RATS AND MICE

Many people will skip this section! Like most people, I have an ingrained fear of rats and mice. It may be their sudden movements that shock me, or perhaps it is just that rats don't look cute. If they looked more like koalas, perhaps we would love them more. However, rats are fascinating creatures in their own way, and provide an important food source for foxes, stoats, buzzards and barn owls.

Once I accidently picked up a brown rat. While feeding my hens, I put my hand into the feed bin and picked up a rat. Frozen in horror, I held my arm outstretched, unable to let go, while the rat wriggled and turned to look at me. I eventually released him. Even though the rat was clasped in my hand, and was clearly terrified of me, it didn't bite me. I have had a new respect for rats ever since.

BROWN RATS

Brown rats can live in most places and eat most types of food. Their favourite food is seeds and cereals, and most feeding occurs in the hour after sunset and in the hour before dawn. Feeding at other times is more dangerous for rats, which are prey to many species. If you see a rat feeding at other times, it may be a younger or less dominant rat, or one which is particularly hungry.

Like young people practising parkour, rats exhibit a behaviour known as thigmotaxis. This means that they like to run alongside vertical surfaces – for example along the base of a wall. It is not known how they find walls and vertical surfaces during the night, but they probably use sight or their whiskers. It is thought that the shelter of walls protects them from birds, which would like to eat them. Some odd studies have taken place, with rats being fed drugs to calm them (such as Diazepam). These calm rats left the security of their vertical walls and ventured out into the open. So, if you see a rat in an open area, you may not feel relaxed, but the rat is probably very laid back.

Rats dig burrows and have underground pantry areas where they store food. They love to live near a food source (don't we all!) and can live in landfills, cereal fields, buildings and farms. They are very agile, can climb and are very clever.

Males are larger than females, and they like to live in family groups. They breed from March to November, but can breed in the winter too if food is plentiful. Females appear to sing to males using ultrasound while mating. Pet rats have also been known to sing in ultrasound when they lie on their backs and their owner tickles their bellies. So perhaps the ultrasonic singing is a sign of happiness. Females are pregnant for three weeks and can have from one to ten pups. Young rats wean after three weeks and become mature at three months. Studies on rat pups show that they love to play with each other, chasing, running and pinning each other to the ground.

Rats can live up to 18 months in the wild, but over 90% of them die when young. They are the main source of food for barn owls.

A researcher called Sandor Gyorgy Fekete studied the effect of music on rats. You may have heard of the 'Mozart effect'. A study in 1993 showed that playing Mozart to students increased their spatial reasoning ability. Children's toy manufacturers went crazy, producing lots of toys that played classical music, to try to make our children more intelligent. I was pregnant myself in 1996 and remember seeing CDs that you would play to your unborn baby. Amazingly, studies show that newborn babies recognise the songs they heard in the womb.

Of course, classical music has a status as being 'intelligent' music – but subsequent studies in humans showed that all music has a positive result on our spatial abilities, with the band Blur having exceptionally high results.

So next time you're lost, turn off Google Maps and put on some Blur.

Of course, animals also seem to love music. One farmer I know plays the melodeon to his cows. There is a viral Sharon Shannon YouTube video where she plays to a field of cows, and I frequently sing to my horse when out trekking (she loves Abba).

But how does music affect rats? Rats are great at doing mazes, so would the addition of some Mozart music improve their maze-solving abilities? The researchers decided to test it. The rats were played some of 'Sonata for Two Pianos in D Major, K448'. I am listening to it as I write this, in the hope of becoming more intelligent.

But the rats gave it little attention. They continued walking about, standing up on their hind legs, grooming and sniffing each other.

Then the researchers had a brainwave. They realised that rat hearing is different to human hearing. Rats hear at a higher pitch, and so were missing lots of the sounds. In fact, they were missing 33–55% of the music. So, the researchers sped up the music, to make sure that the rats could hear it properly.

Have you ever listened to music played at the wrong speed? It was a favourite pastime of teenagers like myself in the 1980s, who had nothing else to do except mess around with a record player. We played records too fast and too slow, and also backwards, which sounded really creepy.

The rats thought the same about their high-speed Mozart. They startled, immobilised, and acted as if they were in a scene from 'Squid Game'. It freaked them out.

Researchers know that life as a lab rat is very stressful. There are unexpected noises, machines and movement, and the researchers are now looking at music that calms people (they are currently trying out Bach's 'Goldberg Variations'). They hope to speed up this music so rats can hear it, and hopefully it will relax rats too. This might improve animal welfare and relax the rats in their difficult, caged lives.

Although I think rats are great, they can carry Weil's disease. Perhaps this is what makes us most scared of them. However, pigs, cattle and dogs can also carry Weil's disease, and we tend not to run screaming from them – an outing to the countryside could become very alarming! Luckily, you can vaccinate your dog against this disease, but there is no vaccine for humans. However, I understand why people might want to get rid of rats.

So, what can we do to deter rats? To start with, stop feeding them. Have a look at where they might be getting food. If it is from a birdfeeder, grease the pole to stop them climbing up, or put an upside-down bowl or broken umbrella midway up the pole. Rats are clean animals, and you can deter them by putting strong-smelling liquids (like Jeyes fluid) around their runs and tunnels. The horrible smell will make them move away.

Attracting other wildlife will reduce the number of rats and mice in the area. When fox numbers increase on our farm, we have very few rats and mice. Buzzards and barn owls eat a lot of rats too!

To catch rats, I use a live trap. I then move them to a cereal field on my farm, a few hundred metres away. My daughter has discovered that if you sing to them while moving them, it calms them down completely. If you must kill them, use the death by chocolate method – put some chocolate on a break-neck trap. If I had to go, I would like to die suddenly while tucking into a delicious chocolate cake. Please don't poison them. Rats have been used for many years as experimental creatures to test drugs on for humans. If their bodies are so like ours, it is likely that they feel pain like we do, and poisoning is a cruel and horrible death. In addition, a barn owl, a fox or your pet cat could find the rat, eat it and end up poisoned too.

Rats use pee to mark everything. They appear to pee constantly and use this marking as we use our mobile phones – to chat to each other, to find out what's going on and to find a mate. Adult males seem to pee the most, especially if a female is around. Smell my aftershave! If the female is impressed, she will mark the male with pee, and then find him by her own scent again a few days later when she comes into heat. It's like leaving traces of your perfume on a man!

Rats mark more when other rats are nearby, and they like to mark their own stuff with their own personal smell. Just as I have lavender in the diffuser in my bedroom, each rat has its own smell, and feels comforted by having this smell in its own place.

Young rats don't really know what to eat and tend to eat foods that smell like their siblings' and mum's breath. In addition, older rats can mark food sites. The younger rats then know it is safe to eat food from that place. Like a Michelin star, the pee attracts the younger rats to the lovely, clean restaurant.

BLACK RATS

This rat is smaller, with big eyes and ears, and is not likely to come to your garden. It is very rare in Ireland and is listed as vulnerable on Ireland's Red List for mammals. This means there is a high possibility that this mammal will become extinct. It is found on Lambay Island off the coast of Dublin, and may be our rarest Irish mammal.

WOOD MICE

This small mouse has large eyes and looks impossibly cute. It has a long tail and long hind feet, and lives in burrows in fields, hedgerows and woodlands. It is clearly into interior design and deposits carefully placed twigs and leaves in definite locations around its territory. The female has a set territory, while the male's territory may overlap with several other mice. Males roam far and wide in search of love in the mating season.

Wood mice like to groom each other, and in the cold winter months, they often nest together to keep warm. They eat seeds, plants, berries and insects, and apparently can even eat small frogs. Just like humans, females seem to like vegetarian food more than males, but seeds seem to be an acquired taste, as young wood mice avoid them until they are older. My children don't like seeds either.

Wood mice are only in oestrus for four hours, so they have to be quick! Peak breeding occurs from June until August. Pregnancy takes three weeks, and DNA analysis has shown that a litter can have several fathers. Wood mice have 4 to 7 young, which leave the nest after around 3 weeks.

Wood mice only live for around 12 months, as foxes, owls and just about everything else preys on them.

HOUSE MICE

You have probably seen this little guy, scurrying across your kitchen floor at nighttime. They can run fast – up to 12km per hour. You probably already know this, having spent fruitless hours chasing them! They live in buildings of all sorts – factories, farm buildings, warehouses and homes – sheltering in cracks and crevices below the floorboards or in the walls, where they make nests of grass, paper and even cloth. It is thought that they attached themselves to people and came to Ireland with Iron Age settlers.

House mice are brown or greyish, with small eyes and long whiskers, and communicate a lot through smell. Anyone who has had a house mouse in their house knows the smell of one! They can also squeak and squeal, and use ultrasound to sing lullabies to their babies. Males also sing ultrasonic love songs to females to make a good impression.

Like myself, they like the comfort of a warm, cosy house, and don't survive well in the rough and tumble of an outdoor life. Outdoors they are often eaten by cats, foxes and stoats, or they can be killed by the cold. Indoors is cosier and much less dangerous. They generally have small territories, rarely going more than 15 metres from their nests.

They are an opportunistic omnivore – meaning they will eat whatever is available. However, they must be listening to the dieticians from 'Operation Transformation', because if given a choice, they will take a little bit of food from lots of different sources – unlike ourselves, who would probably be happy just to eat chips all day long. Their favourite food is cereals, but they will also eat fruit, insects and odd scraps from your floor.

House mice can have between 5 and 10 litters per year, each of 4 to 9 pups. These wean after 2 weeks. Mice seem to become sexually mature when they reach a certain weight, rather than when they reach a certain age.

Rats and mice have been used for generations in lab experiments. In return for food from us, they have suffered discomfort, stress and pain, and have provided us with many medicinal and scientific breakthroughs. We owe them a lot. The very least we can do is trap them humanely in our houses and return them to the wild.

Removing house mice from your home

- Block any holes where mice may be getting in. Mice can get through very small holes – about 17mm, which is just slightly larger than the thickness of a biro. You may have heard the myth that mice have no bones – that they are made of some sort of jelly. Of course, this is not true, but mice have amazingly flexible ribs, which allow them to wiggle through tiny spaces. If their head can fit through, so can their body. Many children have tested this ability on themselves. When my husband was a child, he put his head through railings. Unfortunately, his body couldn't follow, and he was stuck. How wonderful it would be to have flexible mouse ribs.
- Make sure that all your food is kept in sealed containers.
- If all else fails, use a live trap. We use trip traps every year when mice come into our house. They are made of brown plastic and work every time. It is important to check the traps very regularly, as mice can become stressed when confined. And sometimes you might catch something odd like a shrew. Shrews die within a few hours if not released! Now take your mouse on a walk, leave him some food, and release him. It's always great to release any wild animal – a *Born Free* moment!

Attracting mice and rats to your home

- I realise this is not something most people want to do, and I wouldn't advise it unless you have a large farm or somewhere that is free from people. But I know an avid birdwatcher with a bird hide near a large box with small entrances for mice. He fills the box with grain. And each night he watches the barn owl sitting on the box, waiting for mice to come.

Ratty and mousy activities for children

- Make Mum or Dad the rat. Using a washing up liquid bottle, with water and food colouring inside, make a rat pee run. Bring the trail along an obstacle course, jumping over pots, crawling under branches, ending up at the ratty food site for some treats. Then get the kids to follow the trail.

SQUIRRELS

The red squirrel may be our most beautiful mammal. It is a native species, but almost became extinct in the seventeenth century, when most of the trees in Ireland were cut down. It was reintroduced in the nineteenth century, and many of the squirrels we see today come from these original few.

How can we tell red from grey squirrels? You would imagine that it would be easy – one has red hair, and one has grey, right? But often reds have slightly grey hair and greys have brownish-red hair. A friend of mine worked in Wales looking at the distribution of red and grey squirrels. She used hair traps to identify each species. The squirrel runs through a tunnel to get some nuts. The tunnel has sticky tabs

93

attached with Velcro, and hairs from the squirrel stick to the glue. Hey presto, you look at the hairs and see if they are red or grey. But it wasn't so easy. Many hairs were some gradient between grey and red, and others were two-tone. DNA analysis gave a more precise result, but this was a much more expensive way to separate the species.

The red squirrel is half the size of the grey – but as Dougal from 'Father Ted' discovered, it is difficult to judge size when something is far away. It's even harder when an animal is far away and high on a tree. A distinctive difference between the squirrel species is hairy ear tufts, which belong to red squirrels but not greys.

Red squirrels spend most of their time in the treetops, while greys spend a lot of time on the ground. Both species nest in dreys, which are football-shaped and made with sticks and leaves. They generally have moss inside to make it cosy, and are often found in forks of trees, against the trunk. Squirrels may use several dreys, which are shared with other individuals – a sort of time-share community hostel.

Red squirrels have long fingers and claws, and a double-jointed ankle. All these features make them excellent at running up and down trees. They use a range of signals when they are worried, such as shaking their tails or stamping their little feet.

Squirrels eat seeds, flowers and fungi – apparently red squirrels really like dried fungi, and will carry mushrooms into trees and let them dry out for a few days before eating them to get the full gastronomic experience. They also cache food, burying it underground, like a subterranean fridge. Of course, any uneaten seeds have now been neatly planted underground, and will grow into trees and bushes. In this way, squirrels help to spread forests.

Red squirrels love jumping from tree to tree. They are not happy running along the ground, preferring to travel along the branches and crowns of trees. So, they need corridors of trees to connect their habitat – single trees are just too frightening for them.

HOW HAS THE GREY SQUIRREL TAKEN OVER FROM THE RED?

Until recently, the grey squirrel had taken over most of the habitat of the red squirrel, pushing its smaller relation west of the River Shannon. How was this happening?

If you have ever eaten a tea bag, you will know that it makes you sick. And it tastes disgusting too. This is due to the tannins in tea. Acorns have a high level of tannins too. They taste bitter and act as an anti-nutrient, preventing the red squirrel's digestive system from absorbing important nutrients. For red squirrels, an acorn is the opposite of a vitamin tablet – instead of giving nutrition, it takes it away. But somehow the grey squirrel can eat acorns without being affected, and so has an extra food supply around oak trees.

Grey squirrels are also bigger and braver on the ground, and so can eat a wider range of food and can push red squirrels out of good feeding areas.

And then there is squirrel pox. Grey squirrels seem immune to this disease, while the poor reds go blind and die quickly.

But things are changing – The reds have called in a super-hero in the shape of the pine marten. It is not known how pine martens are getting rid of the grey squirrels – but once they move in, grey squirrels vanish. I have witnessed it myself on my farm.

It was thought that the pine martens must be eating the grey squirrels. This is a good theory – the red squirrels are much smaller than the greys and could escape to the tops of trees and along fragile branches if chased by pine martens. So, the pine marten could catch the greys, but not the reds. There has been much analysis of pine marten scats to see if this theory is true. But it has been difficult to find remains of grey squirrels in pine marten poo.

Another theory is the 'landscape of fear' idea. Imagine that a convicted serial killer comes to live next door to you. You are terrified. You worry and fret about it endlessly. You lose your appetite. The stress lowers your resistance and makes you ill. You might decide against having kids. You might move to a new house. All of this happens – even if the monster next door never raises his gun.

A similar thing happens to animals when a predator is around. And this may be what is happening to grey squirrels when the terrifying pine marten comes to join them in the trees.

The pine marten has helped the red squirrel, with greys now living mostly in our cities and the reds reclaiming the rest of the country.

A YEAR IN THE LIFE OF A SQUIRREL

When I was in school, I learned that squirrels hibernate. But it turns out that this is just fake news. They don't hibernate, but they do hang around cosily in bed a little more in wintertime. Females come into heat between January and March and can be chased around trees frantically by lots of males. I have seen this myself, and it is very dramatic. The squirrels only have romance on their mind, and it looks like a high-speed car chase between boy-racer males among the upper branches of the trees. At every moment you expect a disaster to happen.

However, the females find all this excitement attractive, and may mate with several males. The young are born 38 days later, in spring. In times of plenty, she may come into heat again between May and July.

Squirrels are like couch-surfing hippies and are generally easy-going about sharing their homes. In fact, a squirrel doesn't often defend a territory. But this all changes when young arrive. Human mothers are very protective of their young, and the squirrel is no different. She won't allow any other squirrels near, absolutely refusing to share her section of the forest. The male plays no part in raising the young.

Most squirrels have 2 to 5 young, which start to wander outside at around 9 to 10 weeks.

As the young start to wean and become teenagers, the mother often builds herself a resting platform and spends a bit of time away from them, napping and relaxing. It's her 'spa day' experience.

Their food feast happens in the autumn, when squirrels spend hours each day gathering, eating and storing food. But unfortunately, up to 80% of the young can die within the first year, mainly of malnutrition. It's difficult to make it through the winter.

We were lucky to be chosen as a release site for 2 rescued red squirrels. The sisters came from Wildlife Rehabilitation Ireland, and we named them Scarlet and O'Hara. They lived in an outdoor pen for 2 weeks before release, and we had the joy of watching them every day, chasing each other around the pen. They really loved peanuts in their shells, and would sit in hanging baskets, munching away.

But after a while, Scarlet, who was the bigger one, started to do constant backflips. She was really athletic, and it was amazing to watch, but we worried that it was a repetitive behaviour. Many animals show repetitive behaviour patterns when they are stressed.

Take a look next time you are in a zoo or stables, and see if the animals are weaving their heads, rocking, biting or licking bars, pacing, overgrooming or twisting their necks around. These are all signs of unhappiness. In severe cases, they start eating their own excrement or develop a form of bulimia and start vomiting. If you see any of these behaviours, it's time to take action!

The squirrel cage was large, so we added lots of extra branches and hanging baskets for swinging on. They also had two squirrel boxes to hide in – one was purpose-built, and one was an old cajon drum that was upcycled, and which they loved.

This worked for a few days, then the backflipping started again. It was time to release them. We opened the cage, and they came out and immediately made for the forest. The forest is large, and my chances of seeing them again are small, but we still look out for them every day.

Attracting squirrels to your area

- Plant trees that are close together, to allow the red squirrel to move along the treetops. Scots pine, larch, hazel, apple, damson, walnut and beech trees provide food for squirrels. Dog rose is popular as a hedge, with squirrels enjoying the rose hips.

- Buy or build a squirrel feeder and fill it with hazelnuts (with their shells on), walnuts or almonds every few days. The feeder should have a lid on it that only squirrels can open. Squirrels can also eat peanuts and fruit like pears, apples and plums. Some people recommend putting out a cuttlefish bone to provide extra calcium for the squirrel. It is particularly important to feed between June and August, when there are no shoots and buds to eat, and the seeds and nuts have not yet arrived.

- Don't feed the squirrels if there are grey squirrels around. They could transmit squirrel pox to the red squirrels via the feeder.

- Build a squirrel den box – instructions can be found here: *britishredsquirrel.org/wp-content/uploads/2018/04/Red-Squirrels-In-My-Garden-Wales.pdf*

Squirrelly activities for children

- Imagine that you are a red squirrel and want to stay in the treetops. Bring the kids climbing trees in your local park and imagine where you could, and couldn't, go. Or if you are feeling braver you could take the kids on a zipline tree exploration. There are several in Ireland, including in Lough Key Forest Park in Roscommon, Loughcrew in Meath and one in Waterford. You will come home exhausted, with an appreciation of the bravery and muscle power of squirrels.

SMALLER BIRDS

When I started writing about birds, I thought I might call this section 'The Good, the Bad and the Ugly', because that's how people think of birds! If you happen to be a small, cute and almost affectionate bird like a robin, everyone will love you. You will get bird tables, food and water and your photograph on Christmas cards.

But suppose you are a seagull and fancy a bag of chips (and let's face it, who doesn't?). Perhaps you see someone carelessly dropping a few … you might try a small robbery to relieve the owner of his greasy bag. It's almost impossible for me to walk past someone who has a bag of chips. The smell of hot chips and vinegar really makes me want to mug them. And the seagull, whose life depends on getting daily food, can get carried away and might grab the bag. These birds are then labelled as bad – aggressive animals that are terrorising people. In fact, they should be labelled as 'hungry'. In their own way, they are doing their small bit to help us fight our obesity levels.

Then there's the ugly. These are the birds classed as nuisances – pigeons, crows and magpies. I'm delighted to have an encounter with nature and am really thrilled when I'm waiting for a bus at a bus station and a pigeon comes up to share my sandwich. The time passes quickly, as the pigeon and I try to figure each other out. At all times I carry a biscuit in my handbag, just so I can have this type of interaction. But these birds are labelled as dirty and annoying, and when you google them, you will find lots of articles with titles such as 'How to Get Rid of Pigeons'.

We must get beyond the point where we base our judgements and protection of animals on the way they look. It's easy to see why the spectacular giant panda should be saved, but people are laughed at when they try to protect the Kerry slug. The amazing TD, Tony Gregory, was ridiculed in the media when he asked a question in the Dáil about the protection of bats. In fact, he was ahead of his time. So have a think about your perceptions of animals and take a second glance at the ugly ones. There is more to them than meets the eye.

BLUE TITS

This is one of the most common birds found in Irish gardens. It loves peanut feeders, and if you put one out, you will be sure to get a blue tit visiting. I love the fact that this bird likes hanging around in a gang in wintertime. It will team up with finches and other tits, and they will all fly around in a big flock. Just like us when we are doing the Christmas shopping.

Blue tits really need good weather when their young are hatched. In Britain in 2016, blue tits had a really bad summer – records from gardens showed them at their lowest numbers since 2003. This seems to be because of all the rain in springtime, when the birds were fledging. Blue tit parents like to feed their young with insects, particularly moth caterpillars, and there are less insects around when it rains.

A YEAR IN THE LIFE OF A BLUE TIT

The female blue tit seems to have all the power in the mating game. Like a diva, she is courted by the male, who shows her a selection of nice nest sites – equivalent to the '*I have good land with road frontage*' chat-up line. The male has to look good too. Studies show that females fancy males with long wings and good ankles. Bird-ringers often say that blue tits take a really strong hold on their fingers when they are ringing them. Perhaps this is the result of many years of selective breeding, where the guys with the fancy footwork get the girls.

And there are attractive features that we can't see. Male blue tits have ultraviolet shading on the crown feathers of their heads. Along with the long wings and good legs, this makes them irresistible.

The female finally chooses a male and a nest site, but it's all downhill for her from there. She builds the nest alone, using moss, fur and wool to keep it cosy. It takes 1 or 2 weeks to build. Then she lays 8 to 12 eggs. It must be exhausting.

Gardens provide less insects than woodlands, so broods in gardens are generally smaller than those in woods. And she has trouble keeping the eggs warm. Feathers are great for insulation (anyone with a feather duvet can vouch for this). But she is small, and warmth is prevented from escaping from her body by her feathers. So she plucks out the feathers on her belly, creating a 'brood patch'. She puts this patch against the eggs, and the heat of her body acts like a hot water bottle against the eggs, keeping them warm.

The male does his part, bringing her food for two weeks while they wait for the eggs to hatch.

Towards the end of May, the chicks hatch. This should coincide with the peak season for caterpillars, but with global warming, caterpillars are hatching earlier, and now their peak time no longer coincides with when they are needed for the chicks. This can lead to problems with their food supply. Each chick can eat up to 100 caterpillars per day – if you ever watch a nest box, you will be astonished at the number of visits the parents make with food. It's like a non-stop fast food delivery service – you have to admire their parenting skills.

When the fledglings are 18 to 21 days old, the parents call them out of the nest. This is a dangerous time for them, as they tend to sit around on the grass looking cute, or crash through the air. Many young birds die, but if they survive, they often reach three years old. Some blue tits have been found with rings that show they have lived for ten years.

Attracting blue tits to your garden

- Put up a peanut feeder. They will love it.
- Put up a nest box. Blue tits prefer nest boxes with round holes of about 25mm. Unfortunately, this is about the size of the opening in a cigarette bin. In Britain they have been found nesting in these – with disastrous, incendiary results.
- Remember that the chicks are mostly fed on insects, with moth caterpillars being a special favourite. Allow a clump of nettles to grow. This will bring the caterpillars, and food for the chicks.

- The female blue tit has huge calcium demands on her body during the egg-laying season. You can provide calcium in the form of a cuttlefish bone. An easier way is to crush up eggshells, put them in the bottom of your oven to allow them bake, and put them out for the blue tit. Uncooked shells are not a good idea, as they can transmit salmonella (the same reason why we avoid eating raw hens' eggs).

HOUSE SPARROWS

When I was a kid, house sparrows were everywhere. I lived in Dublin and saw them in the back garden most days. So it came as a shock to me to learn that the numbers of sparrows in rural England have fallen by 50% since the 1960s. In the cities it is even worse, with numbers down by 60%.

The numbers in Ireland have declined too. We don't really know why this is happening. There are less stubble fields for sparrows to feed on in rural areas, and this may be one reason. But that would not explain the decline in urban areas. Perhaps air pollution is a cause. Or perhaps we are becoming tidier, with less food waste being dropped on our streets. This decline is happening throughout the world, and for that reason, the house sparrow is on the Amber List of Irish Birds of Conservation Concern.

House sparrows are very social birds and like to hang out together. Tests were done to see how sparrows would react when paired with familiar and unfamiliar sparrows. The birds were put into a strange place (an indoor aviary) and were watched. You can probably guess what happened to the females when put together in a strange location with a female friend. Like women everywhere when on an adventure with a friend, they explored widely and ate well. When the female birds were released with an unknown female, they were initially cautious, but with time began to relax, explore and eat. Bonding between two female sparrows took about an hour. Any woman who has struck up a random friendship with a stranger in a lift can tell you how this works. In no time, they are visiting cafés together.

The males were different – whether with a friend or a stranger, they went off exploring happily. They may have been discussing football. Male sparrows took more risks and were curious about their new domain. The males choose their nest sites, and for this they must naturally be curious, even when in a new and possibly dangerous situation. I have no sense of direction, and am happy to follow my husband around when exploring. Female sparrows do the same, often following males around – especially when the females are hungry!

Other research has found that when sparrows hang out together, they mostly like to join flocks with their siblings. They seem to get along perfectly with their families.

A YEAR IN THE LIFE OF A SPARROW

House sparrows are very sociable, and generally don't defend a territory. They are the apartment dwellers of the bird world, happy to live closely together. They nest under ivy and in gaps in buildings, and are often found using nest boxes.

Sparrows mate between April and August, and they may have 2 to 3 clutches. The female lays 2 to 5 eggs, which are grey/white with fabulous brown speckles. The couple remain loyal to each other and to their home nest site forever. However, they are optimists – if one partner dies, the remaining partner will team up with a new mate within days and will then stay with them for life. Till death do them part!

Parenting is shared between mum and dad, and they both incubate the eggs, which hatch between 11 and 14 days. The chicks are very susceptible to cold and can't control their temperature until they are around 11 days old, which leaves them vulnerable to cold-weather spells. Having a warm parent around is key to their survival.

Although adult sparrows generally eat seeds, the young are mostly fed on insects, including beetles, caterpillars and aphids. The young start to leave the nest after 14 days. They then spend some time figuring out their surroundings, but they still can't feed themselves for another 2 weeks. Superdad steps up, with the male taking over feeding of the fledglings, while the mother spends her time spring cleaning the nest and laying a second set of eggs.

In autumn, the young may gather in a flock – equivalent to our 'post-Leaving Cert holiday', and towards the end of the season, they are joined by the adults, who presumably spoil all the fun. Then the flocks break up and return home. Sparrows usually live within a range of less than five miles and come back to the same nest site each year. So, take a closer look at your house sparrow and its mate. It may have been watching you for several years.

Attracting sparrows to your garden

- Put up a nest box, or better still a row of them, as sparrows like to live together. The circular nest hole entrance should be around 32mm.
- Grow ivy along walls. This provides shelter, nest sites and food for the birds.
- Put out seed feeders.
- Grow nettles for caterpillars and mustard for aphids. The young chicks will munch them up!

STARLINGS

My daughter used to keep guinea pigs as pets in our front garden. They would often escape and charge into the bushes. And when searching for them, I would hear their little voices coming from treetops. Had they learned to fly? No, when I looked up, I would find a starling, doing a perfect guinea pig voice imitation. These birds are amazing at impressions, and can apparently do chainsaws, telephones and a range of other noises.

Ireland may not seem an ideal place to take a winter holiday, but starlings would disagree. Many thousands of them come from northern and eastern Europe every year to join our resident Irish birds for a winter break. In springtime, they fly long distances home again. And over winter, before they roost at night, they form murmurations. These are spectacular, and I would advise you to search for a murmuration in your area. At dusk, the birds gather, chatting and getting excited. If you follow a small group, you will see it joining up with a bigger group, until suddenly, there are thousands of birds, singing and swirling together. The Electric Picnic festival in the skies.

Why do they do it? Some researchers think it could be to do with conserving heat – when you all meet and then roost together, it's warmer. But recent research has shown that it may be an anti-predator strategy – as anyone knows when walking home late at night, it's safer to be in a group than alone. And when a predator attacks, the birds can all suddenly drop out of the skies onto trees together. This will confuse the predator. But you have to wonder what happens. Which bird gives the signal to drop? And how do thousands of birds know how to instantly react?

A neighbour of ours, Gordon, spent several days following our local starlings, until he discovered the murmuration. He took us there to watch, and it was one of the most amazing things I have ever seen. Hundreds of thousands of swirling birds filled the sky, circling and calling. Then they were suddenly gone, to a small copse of trees.

Many flying creatures do this, circling in the sky before bedtime – crows and bats do it too. It really seems to me that it has a social function, a last catch up with all the gossip before bedtime. If I could talk to animals, I would love to know what they are saying in a murmuration. I would spend happy hours circling, chatting and singing with them. It could take some time …

A YEAR IN THE LIFE OF A STARLING

Starlings eat earthworms, snails, beetles and leatherjackets. Leatherjackets are the larvae of the cranefly or daddy long-legs. Research in Scotland showed that 80% of the food given to chicks was leatherjackets. The decline in starling numbers may have something to do with a decline in leatherjackets. Every daddy long-legs is precious! However, starlings can also eat other insects, as well as seeds and fruit.

The male starling starts building a nest and shows it off to potential mates. If the female is impressed by his building skills, they will mate. Then they will both take over the remaining build. However, the female can have strong interior design preferences of her own and may throw out twigs and plants, replacing the bachelor-pad look with soft wool and hairs. Here she will lay 5 to 7 pale blue eggs.

How can you tell male and female starlings apart? Both have long yellow bills, but the difference is easy to remember – the male has blue at the base of its bill, and the female has pink. But I bet you won't notice. Once you start looking at starlings' colour, you will see that they have a glittery sheen to their feathers. The iridescence is startling – it looks as if a rainbow is sparkling on their feathers, with metallic-looking greens and blues.

Researchers in the university of Akron in America looked at the cells in these feathers. Melanin is the skin pigment which makes our skin, eyes and hair darker. The researchers found that cells in iridescent birds have melanosomes (the part of the cell responsible for production of melanin) that are laid down in straight lines. Birds with a matt black colour have melanosomes in a disorganised pattern. And what about really glossy birds, which are fabulously shiny but not iridescent? Birds such as the raven have melanosomes that are slightly organised. When we make glossy materials, they are generally smooth – think of a shiny car for example. We find it difficult to make rough surfaces shiny. However, birds have managed to make feathers glossy, and this research may lead to new processes for materials for industry. I can't wait until I can paint my house in starling iridescent blue.

Starlings sit on their eggs for 12 to 15 days, and the young fledge at around three weeks old. The parents continue to feed them for a week or two, and the female may have a second brood. The male may have another brood with a different but nearby female. Needless to say, this causes some squabbles in the community.

Starlings generally live for around 5 years. We could all learn from them – they have perfected getting along together in large communities of different nationalities. One look at their dancing, swirling murmuration and you will want to perfect it too.

Attracting starlings to your home

- Put up a bird box – a starling is large and needs a bird box with a hole size of about 45mm. Holes and crevices in walls and under fascia are also perfect, so leave gaps in stonework where possible.
- Starlings will eat sunflower husks, peanuts and fat balls. They find it difficult to take the feed from seed feeders, so throw some on the ground or bird table for them. Mealworms are great food for their chicks and will be quickly gobbled up.

- Give them a spa experience. Starlings love to bathe together, so put in a birdbath and wait for the splashing!

DUNNOCKS

This bird is probably in your garden, but you may never have noticed it. It seems insignificant, like Clark Kent before he turns into Superman. The dunnock is brown with lines of black through it, and it seems to live a quiet life. You won't see them out bathing with friends as starlings do, or perching on the end of your shovel as robins might. They appear to be more introverted, hiding under bushes and hedges in ones or twos.

But, as is often the case, dunnocks lead a far more interesting life than you would imagine. Even though dunnocks have a shy nature, it turns out that this bird has a fascinating love life. Some birds are monogamous, pairing together for life. But other birds are definitely swingers. Sometimes you can find a pair, male and female, with an extra female. This is called polygamy. Or you can get a female with two males, which is called polyandry.

There is much research on this behaviour. It seems that there can be an Alpha male, who is in charge, and a Beta male, who waits for his chance to mate with the female when Mr Alpha is off feeding. It's a little like *Bridget Jones's Diary*. If Mr Beta doesn't get a chance to mate, he will sometimes smash up the eggs in a fit of pique. If he does get to mate, both males and the female will feed the chicks, which greatly improves their chances of survival. It seems that the female somehow senses this and will lay more eggs if she has two partners, as more chicks are likely to survive.

Of course, the male only wants to take care of his own off-spring, so before mating with her, he pecks at her behind, which causes her to eject any other sperm. This improves the chances that the chicks will be his.

There is yet another mating setup for dunnocks, called polygynandry. This is basically a 'friends with benefits' system, where both male and female mate with a few dunnocks that they know socially. And all of this is probably happening right now, unnoticed, tucked away in your hedgerow!

If you are afraid of spiders, you will love dunnocks, as they eat lots of them. They also eat other insects and earthworms, and in winter will eat seeds. So you will notice them at your bird table. But remember that these birds don't wish to be seen, so will probably be hopping along the ground under the hedge or along ivy.

A YEAR IN THE LIFE OF A DUNNOCK

A dunnock lays 4 to 5 eggs in a nest in springtime. These eggs are small, blue and glossy. The cuckoo often lays its eggs in a dunnock's nest, even though the cuckoo's egg is white and speckled. To our eyes, the eggs seem really different. Other birds have learnt to recognise the cuckoo egg as an intruder and will throw it out of the nest. But for some reason, dun-nocks can't tell the difference between the new egg and their own, and will happily incubate it and feed the cuckoo chick.

The cuckoo chick will then throw all the other chicks out of the nest, so it gets all the food and parental care for itself.

Numbers of the dunnock are in decline, and it is an important bird in its own right, but the decline in cuckoo numbers is catastrophic. So, this little bird is also essential in the protection of our cuckoo.

The dunnock sits on her eggs for around 15 days, and can have up to 3 broods per year. Most dunnocks live for 2 years, though some have been recorded up to 11 years old. So, take a pair of binoculars, point it at the base of the hedge and have a look for this insignificant little brown bird. As they say, it's the quiet ones you gotta watch!

Attracting dunnocks to your garden

- Remember that dunnocks are shy and don't like to be seen, so plant dense hedges.
- Dunnocks will eat seed from feeders and will also eat fat balls. Again, place the feeder in an undisturbed, quiet place.
- Dunnocks love a cosy nest, so if you are clipping your dog, put the hair outside for the birds to take. Don't use human hair, but hair from a pet is perfect.

ROBINS

My mother feeds a robin every day. It hops into her kitchen for a snack. She thinks she has had it for around 12 years. But

I will have to break some bad news to her: it's unlikely to be the same bird each year – and it's also possible that last year's chap was murdered in a singing competition.

We all love robins, because they are so sociable. It is happy to come close, sit on the end of a gardener's shovel, and build its nest in old hats and teapots. There are an estimated 2 million robins living in Ireland.

Strangely, it is the Irish and British robins that are especially friendly to people. The same species avoids people throughout continental Europe. They may have heard of the friendly Irish and decided to give it a go – and it has worked for both them and us.

We all love the look of the robin, with its fluffy red breast. But singing is its speciality. Like your elderly uncle at a wedding, the male robin is one of the first to start singing, and the last to leave the stage. As with many a rock star, singing is his way of attracting females. Males are very aggressive and will try to out-sing each other in a 'battle of the bands'-type competition. They sing against each other, and perch higher and higher, puffing out their red breasts, singing ever louder, and jumping ever higher. It's a little like the Eurovision, with more and more outrageous songs and costumes. But then it turns violent. Up to 10% of males can be killed in fights during these song contests.

It was thought that robins sang at nighttime in cities because the increased light levels confused them. However, new research disputes this. It appears that noise is the problem, rather than light. In cities and towns, cars, planes and people generate large amounts of daytime noise. The poor male robins just can't be heard in daytime. So, robins have started to sing for longer in cities, late into the evening and night. Studies undertaken by Richard Fuller and his scientists in Sheffield monitored noise levels in the city and discovered that the robin had to sing at nighttime, just to be heard. This all-day/all-night singing must be exhausting for the robin – if you have ever spent a weekend at a rock festival, you will remember how tired you were when you got home. Singing, shouting and attracting mates takes a lot of energy.

Males and females can tell each other apart from their songs, and singing clearly has a role in attracting a mate and repelling intruders. Have a closer listen to the robin's song. It may be a love song, a rant or an angry shout. Don't worry if you miss it – the robin will probably stay up late at night to tell you about it all over again.

A YEAR IN THE LIFE OF A ROBIN

Males fiercely defend their territories, but may accept a visitor if she is female! Sometimes it can take a while for him to accept her – as with all of us, it can be difficult to adjust to someone new living in our homes. There can be arguments, and the female has to ensure that the male realises she is a girl! However, as the romance progresses, she builds a nest, while he spends many hours bringing her gifts of food. This food is crucial to her, as she needs to build up her body weight in order to lay eggs.

After all the nest building, wining and dining, she lays 3 to 5 eggs. In Ireland, the eggs are a cream colour, but the American robin's eggs are a spectacular shade of blue, due to pigment from the mother's haemoglobin.

Robins nest under ivy, in cracks and crevices, and in a wide range of manmade structures. I heard of one robin that nested in a cat's skeleton – perhaps finally getting its revenge on the predator. The female is responsible for keeping the young warm, and if she dies, so will her young, as the male does not know how to create a brood patch.

Both male and female are wonderful parents, and will feed their chicks endlessly. They become very maternal, and can feed chicks of other species too – they have been known to feed blackbird and willow warbler chicks in nearby nests. The chicks leave the nest (fledge) after about 14 days, but the fledglings need to be fed by their parents for about another 3 weeks, while their flight feathers develop. Dad takes over the main parenting duties then, while mum spring-cleans the nest to prepare for another clutch of eggs.

When summer is over, the female leaves the male and often goes back to the area where she was born. Next year, she may return to the same male, or try a different romance.

Winters are tough for all birds, but the robin appears to remain plump. Sadly, this is just an illusion. They puff their feathers up, using pockets of air to keep themselves warm, like wearing one of those expensive designer air jackets. But even so, they can lose up to 10% of their body weight each night. A cold spell over a few days can easily kill them.

Luckily, robins will eat from bird tables, enjoying mealworms, meaty scraps, crushed peanuts and dried fruit. I think every robin Christmas card should come with a pack of dried mealworms for the birds that give their faces to the cards. But a pack of dried mealworms in the post to your loved ones would probably mean that you would get no Christmas presents.

Attracting robins to your garden

- Keep a check on sources of noise pollution in your community. Ask for noise pollution measures to be implemented.
- Never throw out an old teapot! Hang it from its handle in a tree, with the spout facing downwards. A robin might just use it to nest in.
- Put up an open-fronted nest box in a discreet place.
- Plant some ivy along bare walls in your community.

WRENS

The wren seems to have boundless energy. It is tiny, but constantly moving and twitching, like a bird that has just swallowed 20 espressos. These birds have a strange white colour above their eye, which makes them look as if they have just had an accident with an eyebrow pencil.

Wrens love to eat spiders, flies, springtails and beetles, and have even been known to try tadpoles. They have a loud voice for their size, and in fact can produce two notes at the same time – a little like having a set of bagpipes in your lungs. This is because they have an organ called a syrinx at the fork where their windpipe goes into their lungs. It is much more efficient than our larynx, so they can make a much louder song, while singing in harmony. If only I could have a syrinx. Imagine a party trick where you could sing two songs at the same time – at high volume! Sing-alongs in pubs would never be the same again.

A YEAR IN THE LIFE OF A WREN

The male wren builds a number of nests, and if the female

likes one, she will move in. Male wrens are very territorial and won't tolerate another male around in the breeding season.

But this all changes in winter, when the tiny birds get cold. In bad weather, up to 25% of wrens die. A solo wren may easily freeze. So, in wintertime, the male starts calling, asking other wrens to come to keep him warm. In Norfolk in England, 61 wrens were found huddling together in a nest box in winter, all trying to stay warm. We have three that huddle together in our shed when it is cold. And this strategy works well for the male, as often a female or two will remain on after the winter, to mate with him in springtime.

Female wrens lay lots of eggs – 8 to 10 in a clutch, which is amazing for such a small bird. Wrens have been seen eating snail shells, and it is thought that these might provide calcium for the female for her own eggshells. Around 50% of the males take a second partner and rear an additional brood nearby.

The eggs are white and glossy with a bronze speckle, and the female sits on them for 12 to 18 days. The female often uses spider egg sacs – the silk bags in which spiders lay their eggs – to line her nest and keep it soft, and the enthusiastic male brings food to the young once hatched. There are stories of over-enthusiastic males bringing food to the eggs before they have hatched. But it's good to be prepared for new-borns!

Both parents feed the young, which fledge between two and three weeks later.

In folklore, the wren has had bad press. It's impossible to understand how such a tiny, defenceless bird came to be vilified in these stories. In one instance, the wren betrayed St Stephen, by flapping its wings. In another, it betrayed the Irish forces, alerting Cromwell with its song. In yet another evil wren story, a beautiful maiden called Cliona seduced men and drowned them, and would then escape by turning into a wren.

The poor wren has paid a stiff price for these works of fiction, with groups of lads called wren-boys murdering wrens, hanging them on sticks and calling to neighbours on St Stephen's day. What a horrible after-Christmas visit! Although the tradition continues in some places, thankfully the wren is left alone, and a fake wren is used on top of a decorated pole.

Attracting wrens to your garden

- Wintertime is crucial for these birds, as they freeze easily. Breadcrumbs, grated cheese and mealworms are all eaten by wrens, but it's best to sprinkle the food on the ground under or close to bushes, as they may not come to an exposed open birdfeeder.
- The nest box should have a hole size of around 3cm – any larger and a bigger bird will be able to get into it. It should be placed 1.5 to 2 metres from the ground.

FINCHES

I'm an untidy person by nature, but I spent last weekend spring-cleaning the house. This was a bad idea – I should have spent the weekend curled up with a book and a large bar of good chocolate. Because one of my chores was to wash the windows – and the dirt on the windows was doing a very effective job of keeping birds away.

Without the dirt, birds can't see the glass, and already I have a casualty – a male chaffinch crashed yesterday. He is hopping around a cage as we speak, with a damaged wing. He is slowly getting better, and can fly a short distance, so I hope to release him in a day or two when he can fly properly. He is surprisingly fast at running, and it took three of us to catch him when he escaped after his first failed test flight.

He is happily eating Nyjer seed and looking out from the rabbit hutch (where I'm keeping him). The rabbit is not impressed with the takeover of his hutch and is peering in at the squatter.

I'm putting stickers on my windows, so that this doesn't happen again. Bird-shaped stickers work well, and you can let your imagination run riot with stickers. I've used small, semi-transparent flowerpots and sun shapes. They keep the birds from crashing, and I think they look great –though my husband says the house now looks like a children's creche.

A YEAR IN THE LIFE OF A GOLDFINCH

The goldfinch looks amazing, with a red/orange head and golden feathers. Because of its beauty, it has often featured in paintings, and was a real favourite of Renaissance painters. Raphael painted the famous 'Madonna of the Goldfinch' in 1505. If any bird would encourage you to whip out the paper and paints, this is the one.

Goldfinches mostly eat small seeds. Thistle seeds and the catkins of alder are favourites, and their legs are especially designed to help them clutch onto the plant while their beak pulls out the seed. They will come to bird feeders or eat off the ground, and love Nyjer and oilseed rape seeds. They also love sunflower hearts.

Their song is a lovely twittering sound. Apparently, goldfinches have a special song for anxiety – a shout of *help! help!* with rising notes as the bird gets more frightened. A group of goldfinches is called a 'charm', and they like to hang around together in flocks, particularly in the autumn.

The male seduces the female by rocking from side to side while singing – much like Mick Jagger. He also moves his wings to show off his gold bars. The combination of gold, singing and dance moves proves irresistible to the female, and she then proceeds to build a nest.

The nest of the goldfinch is delicate, made of mosses and hair, and is placed high in a tree. The female lays around 5 eggs in June, which hatch after 2 weeks. Two to three weeks later, the young fledge the nest.

Attracting goldfinches to your garden

- Plant seed-bearing plants, such as teasel and cosmos. Or just do nothing and let the dock and thistle grow. The most important thing is to leave the seed heads on the plants over winter, for the birds to eat.
- Goldfinches love Nyjer seed. I have often put oilseed rape in Nyjer seed feeders, as it is cheaper and is grown locally, and the finches love it too.
- Thick shrubbery, trees and ivy are important nesting sites for goldfinches, as they don't seem to like using nest boxes, so be careful with the pruning shears in summertime!

BIGGER BIRDS

JACKDAWS

As I sit in the sun writing this book, two jackdaws are frantically gathering twigs. They plan to build a nest in the shed behind me. It looks like a monumental undertaking, judging by the vast amounts of sticks being collected and sorted.

I can't tell one jackdaw apart from another, but the two jackdaws behind me probably know me personally. They can tell individual humans apart. Researchers have studied jackdaw curses – or 'scolding calls' as they are known by the scientific community. They played these pre-recorded scolding calls to the birds, as a person walked by their nest. Imagine you saw a person walking by your house, and then heard a bloodcurdling scream. What would you do? The birds reacted as we would – first by looking in their nests to check that their young were okay, and then by calling their friends (with a 'mobbing' call) to gang up and drive the intruder away.

To see if the jackdaws recognised individual human faces, the scientists wore masks when checking nests and weighing fledglings. Although no harm was done to the chicks, this caused great concern to the jackdaw parents, who saw their nests and young being raided by Halloween-type masked researchers. It probably also looked alarming to any humans passing by.

The next time the scientists wore the masks, the jackdaws shrieked and yelled, even though the scientists were not near the nest. Think of all the great robbery films you have watched in the past. Now imagine, you are in your village, visiting the bank. Suddenly three guys in balaclavas walk in. They may only be lodging some money, but I bet you will not wait to find out. Like the jackdaws, you will be outside, shrieking and yelling.

A YEAR IN THE LIFE OF A JACKDAW

Jackdaws are found throughout Ireland, but they avoid open mountains. They are very intelligent, social birds, which live in groups and can be easily seen as they feed in the open over fields and parkland. They will eat fruit, seeds, insects and small mammals.

But their speciality is in the art of romance. Valentine's day cards have hearts on them, but I think this is a mistake. Every Valentine's Day card should have a jackdaw painted on it. Like Italian men, jackdaws are experts in the language of love.

The male brings gifts of food to the female throughout the year. The female rarely feeds the male, but will often sit together with him, touching and preening him. They forage together for food and help each other out in conflicts with other birds and predators.

Status is very important to a male jackdaw, and he spends a lot of time pecking and arguing over it. Males are usually dominant to females, but the if the female pairs with a high-status male, she too becomes a high-status bird. Think of professional footballers and their wives. And this is a great match. The pair remains devoted to each other for life. It really is 'for better or worse', as even if the nest fails, or they fail to breed, they will remain together and try again the next year. Same-sex couples of jackdaws have also been found, both in captivity and in the wild.

Jackdaws like to nest in cavities, chimneys and holes in trees and buildings. Here the females will lay 4 to 5 eggs, which she will sit on for 20 days. The eggs are a speckled glossy blue, and the chicks are fed by the male when they hatch.

The chicks fledge after around 32 days, and jackdaws may survive for 5 years in the wild.

Jackdaws are known to love shiny things. When I had an injured one living with me, it spent many happy hours arranging and rearranging its bling collection of tinfoil. Eventually he looked like a hip-hop artist. However, this love of shiny stuff has been difficult to prove in research projects. Scientists have found that the birds refuse to steal gems while being studied. Perhaps the jackdaws are just spending their time studying us.

Attracting jackdaws to your home

- Jackdaws will try anything – berries, seeds, nuts, fruit, insects, scraps, etc. Throw it all out and see what happens. Our jackdaws love suet balls.
- Leave gaps in old sheds and buildings for nests. Crevices in trees are also important. Jackdaws have been known to nest in tawny owl boxes in Britain, so if you are good at woodwork, you could download a plan and try it out.
  rspb.org.uk/birds-and-wildlife/advice/how-you-can-help-birds/ nestboxes/nestboxes-for-owls-and-kestrels/tawny-owl-boxes

MAGPIES

This bird is often hated by people. Yet it is large and noisy – exactly the type of bird that is ideal for birdwatching. It is easy to spot as it chatters away, busy with its friends. Emily Dickenson called them 'flying frying pans'.

However, this poor bird has a reputation as a sinister murderer, raiding tiny songbirds' nests and eating the chicks and eggs. It sounds so awful. But you may be surprised to learn that the animal that kills most songbirds is probably sitting on your lap right now, purring softly. Cats are lethal predators of songbirds. The decline of hedgerows and other habitats is also causing the decline of small songbirds.

Magpies do eat songbird chicks and eggs, and a team in Britain looked at populations of 15 songbird species from 1966 to 1986. The numbers of magpies increased by about 5% each year, and although magpies did eat eggs and chicks, overall, there was no obvious effect on songbird nesting success. I think magpies are just loud and exuberant, and this makes them an easy target – it's easier to blame a large, boisterous bird than to look at the complex reasons for habitat loss in our cities and rural areas.

We may be cautious of magpies simply because they are so intelligent. If we scaled up a magpie to our size, their brain would be as big as ours. They have been known to use tools in captivity to clean out their cages – just like ourselves with a sweeping brush. And they are the only bird to pass the mirror test. The mirror test is designed to see if we are self-aware – if we know that we exist. Children pass the mirror test about the same time that they develop empathy.

To try the test, you must first put a sticker on the subject (the magpie), in a place they cannot see. Then you give the animal a mirror. First, the animal must realise that the reflection is themselves. Then they have to figure out where the sticker is, and finally, they must remove the sticker. Magpies can do this. Children are usually about 2 years old when they pass the test. You are probably dashing out right now to find a small child to try it on.

Of course, the mirror test is not perfect. Some animals, like gorillas, are very unhappy about making eye contact, so they find it unnerving to look at themselves in mirrors. They will go away quickly from the mirror and remove the sticker later on. Other animals, such as elephants, spend a lot of time splashing mud on their bodies, and probably like having stickers attached, so they won't remove them! And children who are brought up in places without mirrors can be uncomfortable about looking in mirrors – I often feel like that myself. Which of us hasn't had a bad hair day, or month, when we avoided mirrors? If we or other animals fail the mirror test, it doesn't necessarily mean that we lack self-awareness or empathy.

Magpies can store food for later, showing that they can plan ahead, and have been taught to count in captivity. Like the jackdaw, they can recognise faces and can tell dangerous people from safe people. This is a bird I would like to have with me when walking down a dodgy street late at night!

A YEAR IN THE LIFE OF A MAGPIE

Male magpies perform elaborate mating dances, raising and lowering their head feathers and opening their tail like a fan. Their final seductive trick is calling in a soft voice to attract the girls. Once romanced, the female stays with her mate for life. They usually hold a territory of about 12 acres. Although there is a lot of love between the pairs, there does not seem to be a lot of sex, with some studies showing magpies mating just 3 times per clutch of eggs. Many magpies (somewhere between 25% and 60%) don't mate and remain single, hanging around in flocks of friends.

Magpies build large, solitary nests in tall trees, and the female lays around 6 blue-green eggs. These eggs hatch almost 3 weeks later, and the young are born bald and blind. After around a week, they open their eyes. They fledge after 4 weeks, but are very vulnerable and can barely fly for a while, so continue to be fed. They hang around with their parents until September, and then leave home to form flocks.

Magpies tend to eat everything – seeds, roadkill, fruit, berries, eggs – and have been shown to do well near roadways. This may be because their predators are killed by cars, and they can get their revenge by eating this roadkill. It's like living next door to a shopping centre, with kind security guards operating a shoot-to-kill policy on your enemies.

Attracting magpies to your home

- Plant tall trees for them to nest in.
- Throw out your kitchen scraps to the magpies (except very salty food)! Magpies chop up large food items for their young,

so there is no chance of them choking. And remember, the magpies can recognise you, can count what you are giving them, and probably have the self-awareness to be grateful!

ROOKS

I love the shiny, blue-black feathers of a rook, and how it can open almost any birdfeeder. Its intelligence has been well researched. Dr Christopher Bird and Dr Nathan Emery from the Queen Mary University of London designed some tasks to test whether rooks could use tools. The first one involved a dish with food, floating on water at a level too low for the rook to reach.

The famous scientist Archimedes discovered that if you drop weights into water, the water displaces by the same amount. It took years for people to figure this out, and the story goes that Archimedes was lying in his bath when he realised it (probably with bathwater swooshing over the side onto the bathroom floor). He was so excited, he jumped out and ran naked around Greece, telling everyone about it. It must have been worrying for the Greeks to have a naked, wet scientist running around spouting mathematical theories, but at least it made science interesting.

So, could the rook discover something that people took centuries to figure out? Like Archimedes in his bath, the rooks had a 'Eureka' moment, and dropped in stones to raise the water level. Then they ate their treat (with a lot less fuss than Archimedes).

Now the scientists made the problem more difficult. They provided stones that wouldn't fit. The rooks had to use two tools – one large stone to put into a tube, which released a smaller stone, which could fit into another tube – and release the treat. Hey presto! No problem to the intelligent crow.

At this point, I think the rook should have simply been awarded a doctorate, but instead the tasks were made even more difficult. In a bird puzzle worthy of 'Mastermind' (*'Hello, I'm a rook, representing the Queen Mary University of London'*), a small bucket was placed within a large bucket. The small bucket had a treat in it, but was too far away to reach. The rook made a tool out of a piece of wire, hooked the small bucket and pulled it up. Until recently, it was thought that only chimpanzees could use tools, but these studies show that rooks have this ability too. Their tool-making skills are better than my own.

A YEAR IN THE LIFE OF THE ROOK

With a voice like Rod Stewart, singing is very important to rooks. Over 20 different calls have been recorded, and there is much chattering between males and females. A pair will often sing a duet together while foraging for food and building their nest of sticks and twigs, often in a tall tree. It is thought that this singing helps strengthen their bonds. The male also shows off by bowing and fanning his tail.

The adults like to stay close to home and they are early nest-ers, laying eggs in late February and early March. Because of this, it will be interesting to see what effect climate change will have on their food supply, and in Britain this is being monitored closely. If the seasons change, perhaps food will not be available for their chicks when they need it.

Rooks mate for life, and the female lays 3 to 4 eggs, which hatch after about 2 weeks. While she is sitting on her nest, brooding the eggs, she often makes pathetic-sounding begging calls to her mate. Scientists originally thought that it was because she was hungry and was asking him for food. However, even when she has just eaten, she still makes the begging sounds. Perhaps she is lonely, or – like most new mums – suffering from the effects of being cooped up at home. Minding eggs is not as easy as it looks for a highly sociable bird.

The chicks stay in the nest for a month before they fledge. Adult rooks have a grey-white area of bare skin around their nostrils and chin, but the young don't have this, so it is possible to age them. Rooks breed after 2 years and usually live for 6 years, though one was found with a ring on it in Britain that showed it was almost 23 years old.

The adults tend to perch high up on the tree, with the youngsters below, and in autumn, the young leave to explore the world – they can travel 100km from their home-bound parents.

Attracting rooks to your area

- Plant tall trees. If you can't fit one in your garden, ask the local council if you can plant a few on a nearby green area. Rooks need trees to nest in, and also to perch in while they check the ground to see if it is safe to land.

- Put out food and water. Rooks will eat most food, but love peanuts, eggs, sunflower seeds, worms and fat balls. They also eat dog and cat food. If the food is hard, they like to soak it in water before eating it, so leave out some water in a bowl. Our local primary headmaster was a kind man and collected the scraps left over from the children's lunches. He would throw them onto a flat-roofed hut. The birds would gather every day for their treat as the children left school. A great way to use food waste.

PIGEONS

When I was small, my parents had fabulous neighbours, Gertie and Jim. We were always in and out of each other's houses, and we used to play with their kids. But Jim had a special treat outside. In an enormous building we all called the villa, he kept racing pigeons, and he would often bring me up to feed and hold these precious birds.

So last year, when I took in a pigeon with a damaged wing, of course we christened it Gertie. Gertie stayed with us for six weeks, until her wing healed and she could fly again. She was full of character, hopping about and cooing to us. She seemed fascinated by people, bobbing her head and spinning. But later we realised that these moves were her mating dance. We had sexed her wrongly. Gertie was actually Jim.

FERAL PIGEONS

I love these birds because they will approach you, often begging for food. Their turned head and sad eyes work on me every time. Other people are not so enamoured by feral pigeons as they perch on apartment ledges, which they see as cliff faces, pooing and generally making a mess.

If you must get rid of pigeons from your balcony or building, please don't kill them!

Slope the angle of whatever ledge they are perching on. If it is plastic, it will need to have a slope of at least 25 degrees. With less slippery wood, the angle will have to be 35 degrees. For concrete, the slope must be 50 degrees. If the ledge is shorter than 4cm, pigeons will not perch on it.

You could put a splash board – a short piece of timber – under their perch, to catch the droppings.

To keep feral pigeons out of a building, make sure that any square entrance holes are less than 6cm x 6cm.

But I hope that you will not take any of the above advice. Our towns and cities are becoming increasingly inhospitable places. While researching this book, I found lots of advice on using spikes to deter pigeons. And then I found horrible articles on using spikes along ledges to deter people from resting there. We need to embrace and cherish everybody – people and nature – within our urban jungle.

Feral pigeons are descended from the rock dove. They became domesticated when people bred them to eat. They are found throughout Ireland, eating scraps, cereals, fruit and the seeds of grasses.

A YEAR IN THE LIFE OF A FERAL PIGEON

Feral pigeons mate for life, and mating involves a lot of flapping of wings. They lay 2 eggs, which hatch 14 days later. They can raise several broods throughout the summer.

If you have spent time watching feral pigeons, you will notice that they are often missing toes. A study in Paris with the Natural History Museum and the University of Lyon looked at these poor pigeons. Feral pigeons suffer from a problem called string-foot. As they live in urban areas, they don't have natural materials to build their nests from, and they pick up our litter – including bits of string, human hair and dental floss. These wrap around their toes, cutting off their blood supply. I bet it is really painful. In the end, the toes fall off.

Paris is a very stylish place, and if you go there, you will notice the glamorous hairstyles. The research group wondered if hair was the cause of all the pigeon's problems. They counted injured pigeons and mapped them locally with the number of hairdressers in a street. Amazingly, they discovered that areas with lots of hairdressers had lots of injured pigeons. To protect our pigeons, we have to ensure that no human hair cuttings escape from the local hairdressers – and keep our streets litter-free.

The researchers also plotted pigeon toe loss against noise and air pollution. Interestingly, areas with greater noise and air pollution had a greater number of pigeons with limb loss. So, if you are thinking of buying a house and are wondering if it is in a good area, perhaps you should spend some time feeding the local pigeons and counting their toes. If all toes are intact, perhaps the area has low levels of noise and air pollution. Or it may just have low levels of hairdressers.

THE WOOD PIGEON

I bought my first house based on the fact that a wood pigeon was living in the garden. If a large, wild bird could live there, then it looked like a good place for me too. The dramatic flapping and cooing completely distracted me from the fact that the house had no running water or toilet. This is a trick that every auctioneer should use.

Wood pigeons are a large, plump-looking bird, with a white neck patch, and they live in most places in Ireland. They make a fabulous 'hoo-woo-woo' sound, cooing as they rise upwards into the air. They make a great deal of flapping noise as they take off.

One amazing fact about all pigeons is that they are the only birds which can suck up water. Most birds bob their heads up and down to scoop up and swallow drinks. Yet we watched Gertie drinking water one day, using her beak like a straw and sucking up her drink. We were amazed, and invited everyone around to see this wonder bird. But it turns out that all pigeons can do it, although it is not known how. The diet of the wood pigeon is very dry, and it needs a lot of water – perhaps this is a very necessary skill.

A YEAR IN THE LIFE OF THE WOOD PIGEON

Wood pigeons eat seeds, berries, leaves, flowers, nuts and buds. They were often hated by farmers, as it was thought that they destroyed crops, but this is a myth, and there is no evidence of any crops being destroyed by wood pigeons.

The wood pigeon is a firm believer in equality of the sexes. Both parents build the nest in April. The female lays 2 eggs, and both male and female incubate them, for around 17 days.

And what happens next is amazing. Once the chicks hatch, the hormone prolactin kicks in. This is known as the love hormone and is produced in high quantities in breastfeeding human mothers, as it helps produce milk. Amazingly, both male and female wood pigeons produce high levels of prolactin – and they both produce pigeon milk! This is not like milk from mammals, as it is produced in the bird's crop. A crop is a sack-like bulge just above the stomach, where most birds can store food. But in pigeons, this sack can produce milk. The milk is lumpy, like cottage cheese, but contains all the wonderful things milk generally contains, such as proteins, fats, antioxidants, good bacteria and a range of magical ingredients that help the chicks' immune systems.

As the chicks get older, the parents mix seeds with the milk – just as we start giving mushy food to babies, until they are weaned. And after 33 days, the pigeon chicks fledge. Many live for 3 years.

Attracting pigeons to your home

- Pigeons are not fussy. They will eat almost anything, but seeds and grains of all types are favourites. Throw the food on the grass or even on your roof.
- Remember that they need water – an old frying pan or dish works really well as a drinker.
- Plant for pigeons. Plants such as elderberries are loved by pigeons – and the flowers make a nice cordial drink for us too.

BUZZARDS

Buzz Lightyear, our buzzard, came into our lives when he was shot. These poor birds have been persecuted for years, and this sad guy was found hopping around a field nearby, near my doctor's surgery. At the time, my husband was there with my son, who had a chest infection. It is probably not wise to drag a sick child into a field to search for a sick buzzard, but both child and buzzard livened up considerably with the chase.

I didn't know anything about the personality of a buzzard, and little Buzz looked as sweet as a budgie, sitting under his heat lamp and eating bits and pieces for us. He seemed almost tame, but his wing was badly damaged.

We sent him off to the Kildare Animal Foundation, where he was treated by the wildlife team. And the animal they sent back to us was very different. Clearly, he had just been docile and compliant because he was really ill. This new bird had attitude! He was no budgie, but a wild, magnificent creature, and would thrash around his cage in horror when we would appear. Buzz Lightyear had changed from a kid's toy into a wild and fascinating animal. We considered renaming him Heathcliff. He was completely mesmerising – I now see how people can be enthralled by birds of prey.

And best of all, he could fly. We released him nearby, and I hope he is doing well.

You have probably seen buzzards sitting on lampposts above motorways, hoping that you will run over some small creature and provide dinner for them. We are only recently seeing buzzards in Ireland again. They have a very boom-and-bust history. They used to be plentiful, but died out in the 1890s. Then some Scottish birds moved to Antrim in 1933 and bred on Rathlin Island. These birds began to repopulate the country, but then suffered a population crash – the rabbits they like to feed on became infected with myxomatosis and died, and the buzzards starved without the rabbits for food.

Next, some more Scottish birds decided to emigrate in 1968, and managed to make a go of life in Northern Ireland. However, Northern Ireland has always had better laws around poison safety than the Republic of Ireland, and it is thought that when the buzzards crossed the border, they would find meat laced with poison and would die.

Strychnine was still legal in the Republic of Ireland until 1991, and only since 2010 is it illegal to poison any animal or bird (except rats and mice). I have even seen poison placed near children's playgrounds. Thankfully, the law is being enforced – if you find poisoned meat or suspect a bird has been poisoned, you can call the NPWS, and they will investigate. But take care – some of the illegal poisons used are lethal to people too, and you can easily get the poison on your hands while examining an injured bird or carcase.

A farmer near Tipperary reported some live pigeons that he had found tethered on his land. Nearby, he found two dead buzzards. He investigated with Birdwatch Ireland and discovered that the pigeons were coated in carbofuran – a powerful neurotoxin that is banned in Europe. Birdwatch say that a quarter teaspoon is enough to kill an adult, and it easily seeps into water supplies. Thankfully the farmer who rescued the pigeons was safe.

With the enforcement of the laws around poisoning,

numbers of Irish buzzards have been increasing. The northern birds have been joined by some Welsh birds, which have flown across the Irish sea. But buzzards are not yet free from persecution. In 2020, 23 buzzards were illegally poisoned in Timolegue. Sadly, the massacre of these fabulous birds continues.

Yet these birds are the farmer's friends. Their main food is rabbits, rats and crows – animals that the farmer wants kept away from his cereal crops. Dr Eimear Rooney from Queen's University studied the diet of buzzards in great detail. In Britain, they often eat greater white-toothed shrews (on the islands on which they occur) and bank voles, but these are in short supply in Ireland, and she wondered what they were eating instead. She looked at 1,194 items of prey brought back to 61 nests, and rabbits, rooks and rats were the favourite dinners. In areas with more rabbits, more chicks survived to adulthood. Rabbit stew was definitely on the menu for the buzzard chick's dinner.

A YEAR IN THE LIFE OF THE BUZZARD

You might hear gentle mewing sounds from buzzards as they travel through the sky. It all sounds very sweet for a bird of prey. But if I was a male buzzard making these sounds, I'd be screaming with fear. To impress the girls, he has to do a 'rollercoaster'. This involves flying high into the sky, then twisting and turning while falling with his mate. Psychologists say that when we have an adrenaline rush, we are likely to feel attracted to someone. That's why they advise us to bring potential dates on rock-climbing adventures. The buzzard seems to have taken this advice, as his dates include highly dangerous acrobatic flying displays. It must work for him, as buzzards mate for life. Personally, a date like that would have me running away.

Buzzards build enormous nests in March, which can be a metre wide and 60cm deep. The female lays 2 to 4 eggs and sits on them for around 33 days, while the male brings her food. The young fledge 50 to 60 days later, but are still fed by their parents for another 6 to 8 weeks. They become sexually mature at 3 years old, but sadly it is thought that 75% of them die before they reach this age.

Attracting buzzards to your area

- It is unlikely that a buzzard will come to your garden, but rabbits, mice and crows will bring them to fields. They also love to eat roadkill.

SPARROWHAWKS

How do you know if your bird table is a success? When a sparrowhawk comes visiting. Most people are horrified as they watch the in-flight murder of small birds they have been feeding throughout the year. But a sparrow-hawk is an apex predator and will only arrive if you have lots and lots of birds. If you see a sparrowhawk, your bird table has been a real success and you should celebrate. The spar-rowhawk is not very successful at catch-ing prey, with a kill just one time out of every ten tries, and usually picks off older, slow or injured birds, ensuring that the most able reproduce.

If you watch a sparrowhawk, you will see it appearing like a fighter aircraft, sleekly twisting and turning among tree branches. It is a true master of flight. It likes to move along woodland edges, and in farmland along hedgerows. A sparrowhawk is often so focused on its prey that it crashes very dramatically.

An interesting study, led by Nora Carlson, placed robotic sparrowhawks among wild blue tits, to see how the blue tits would react. Needless to say, the blue tits became anxious, particularly if the sparrowhawk moved or called. Then the researchers placed a dead and stuffed blue tit in the claws of the sparrowhawk and watched how the blue tits reacted.

Immediately the blue tits began scanning – turning to look at the dramatic scene – as we would start rubbernecking at the scene of a car crash. The researchers thought that the blue tits were checking the predator in an *I'm glad that's not me, and I'll be safe while he's eating her* kind of way. And they felt that the blue tits were peering at the victim, possibly trying to identify it: *Is that Maisie's daughter?*

Sparrowhawks are ambush predators, appearing suddenly out of nowhere to grab a bird and escape into the skies. Although they appear to cause carnage at the bird tables, studies show that there is no real effect on the size of the small bird population if a sparrowhawk is present. So don't worry if a sparrowhawk is visiting your bird feeders. You will continue to have plenty of small birds – and a stunning apex predator too!

A YEAR IN THE LIFE OF A SPARROWHAWK

Sparrowhawks nest in woodland and small stands of trees, at least half a kilometre away from other sparrowhawk nests. They like to keep away from their neighbours.

The female lays 3 to 6 eggs, which hatch over several days around 33 days later. If something goes wrong with their food supply, the chicks hatching over several days helps to ensure that at least some of them will survive. The male provides almost all the food, while the female takes care of the eggs and chicks.

The chicks start to leave the nest at around 4 weeks of age, but come back at nighttime to their home, until their feathers have grown and they have figured out how to hunt.

Attracting sparrowhawks to your area

- Persuade your local council or friendly farmer to plant small patches of trees and woodland to provide nesting areas.
- Feed the small birds with birdfeeders – and wait!

KESTRELS

If you look up and see a bird that appears to be hanging from a piece of string, you are probably watching a kestrel hover. This bird is amazing: like an experienced ballerina, it keeps its head still, while hovering in the air. Unlike most ballerinas, it can suddenly dive on a mouse to catch a quick bite of lunch.

Kestrels have a second superpower. They can see ultraviolet

light, which allows them to follow the urine trails of rats and mice. We have spent many happy hours with our local primary school, where the flapping children pretend to be kestrels, and the adults (mice) run around with washing up liquid bottles full of water with food colouring, jumping over logs and hiding. The kestrel children follow the trails and always find their prey!

A kestrel is about the same size as a magpie and has pointed wings. It can often be seen feeding in the open, and it has excellent eyesight. It eats insects, mice, shrews and sometimes small birds. In Ireland, the kestrel population was estimated at 13,500 in 2016, a decrease of 44.9% between 1998 and 2016, and a 22.1% decrease in distribution over the 25-year period 1991 to 2016. Britain's numbers have fallen by 50% since the 1970s!

If you are lucky, and very observant, you might find a kestrel pellet. It will look like a small, furry dog poo, with a point at one end. A pellet is the undigested remains of whatever the bird was eating, so is a fascinating source of information on the local food supply. The pellet does not pass through the intestine, but instead is regurgitated and spat out. This means that it is not smelly.

Some poking with a stick will reveal the last lunch eaten. Often you will find bits of mouse jaws, and bits of beetles. It is difficult to find pellets in the wild, but you can buy pellets online from the Barn Owl Trust in the UK, complete with a guide to identification of the bits you will find inside.

A perfect Christmas stocking filler!

A YEAR IN THE LIFE OF A KESTREL

If there is a good supply of food, the female kestrel lays 4 to 5 eggs in April or May. In years with poor food supplies, she will not lay eggs. Kestrels don't build nests, but lay their eggs in holes in trees, on ledges or in abandoned crows' nests.

The chicks hatch after a month and, amazingly, there seems to be no sibling rivalry among brothers and sisters. This is very unusual in any family. Perhaps this is their real superpower! The family lives together like 'The Waltons' in peaceful, rural bliss for around 5 weeks, when the young decide to leave home.

Attracting kestrels to your area

- Put up kestrel boxes. These birds like to use readymade nest sites, so it is always good to provide a few. As I write this, there is a kestrel checking out a barn owl box on my farm. I hope she'll move in.
- Don't use rat or mouse poison – you will accidently kill the birds that are eating the mice. Use live traps or breakneck traps.

Attracting birds of all types to your garden

Of course, the best way to attract birds is to feed them. There are a range of feeds available. If you are just doing the minimum, then sunflower seeds and peanuts are a good start. And remember to throw out your food waste for the birds. Birds will eat most food, just remember not to give them anything very salty.

Other feeds include:

- Nyjer seed: You will need a special feeder with tiny holes in it. You will see lots of it scattered on the ground below and wonder if they are just throwing their food about, but in fact you are probably seeing the husks of the seed. Finches love this type of seed, and they open the husk to get at the seed inside.

  I worry about the carbon footprint and food miles involved in importing seed for birds, so I have recently been filling my Nyjer feeders with oil seed rape seeds, which are grown in Ireland. The finches seem to love them, and I see a few stray seeds sprouting on the ground, so I expect to have some pretty yellow flowers below the feeders in summertime.

- Peanuts: Birds love peanuts! You can get enormous sacks of them in most pet shops, and they are full of fats, protein, iron and potassium. You may see pretty feeders that you put jars of peanut butter inside, but birds using these can get oil from the peanut butter onto their feathers, and it impairs their flying. So only buy listed 'peanut butter for birds' jars for these feeders. Or better still, just leave the peanuts whole and in a peanut feeder.

- Suet balls: You can make your own or buy them in bulk. Wrens, jays and thrushes love them. Squirrels and foxes also love to eat them. Put them in large suet feeders or crush them up on a bird table.

- Sunflower seeds: These are one of the best seeds for birds, full of fat, protein and vitamin B. Striped sunflower seeds have a tough husk, and although birds love them, they are a little difficult to open. Black sunflower seeds have a softer husk, and the seeds themselves have more oil (these are the seeds used to make our sunflower cooking oil). This oil is very nutritious.

Sunflower hearts are the insides of both types of sunflower seeds, and although they are more expensive to buy, the birds don't have the effort of extracting the seeds and throwing husks around the garden. Sunflower hearts can be chipped for smaller birds.

- Mixed seeds: The usual rule is, the cheaper the seed, the cheaper the ingredients. Make sure you buy seed mix with a high sunflower or peanut content. Other ingredients like wheat are used as fillers in cheaper feeds. I noticed last night that the birds had knocked down a seed feeder and had eaten everything but the wheat. However, today they are eating the wheat as a last resort.

- Mealworms: Many birds love eating mealworms. However, I don't like the idea of plastic tubs full of poor dead worms, so I avoid using them. Instead, I have made a compost heap of dead leaves, and the birds search for their own insects.

A word about feeding bread: I would be happy to live on white bread and jam forever, but it would not be a healthy diet. This applies to birds too. While it is fine to throw out your waste bread to a collection of birds at the bird table, it becomes a problem if the birds eat only bread. It is likely that the birds in your garden will be eating a range of other foods, so bread scraps should be fine to eat. But white bread is so lovely, that when there is lots of it, the birds will choose it to eat first.

Swans have a particular problem here. If swans eat mostly bread, they will not digest enough other nutrients, and the cygnets can develop a bone malformation called angelwing, which results in the wrist bone being turned. The poor swan has its wings splayed sideways, and can never fly. If you visit swans in large public parks, don't feed them bread, as it is likely that they are getting lots of it already. But it is fine to give bread to birds in small quantities. As with humans, a little of what you fancy does you good.

Other ways to attract birds

- Buy or make a bird bath. It needs to be shallow, so the birds can have a good splash. An old frying pan works well.
- Birds also need to drink – when you are pouring a kettle over the car window to defrost it, remember also to pour a drop to break the ice in the bird bath.
- Keep cats under control, and pets away from the bird area.
- Remove scary garden ornaments – wind chimes, ladders, flapping plastic, etc.
- Clean up litter in your area to avoid string foot in birds.
- Put stickers on large windows to prevent birds from striking them.
- Gardening for birds: Birds need food, water and shelter. A garden pond will provide water and insects to feed on, and layers of hedgerow and shrubs will provide shelter. If you have space, plant a tree. But even if your garden is small, you can still think large. Have a look at your house and see what vertical space can be used. Perhaps you could grow ivy up the walls to provide food and shelter. Or there might be space for window boxes full of wildflower seed. As we concrete over land, we need to think of ways to go high-rise with plants and

animals, and green walls and roofs are an obvious answer. You can buy plant pockets – strips of material with hanging pockets. They look a little like pocket shoe organisers. You attach them to the wall, add some compost and seeds, and you have an instant green wall.

Fruit bushes and bushes with berries will be popular with birds – and with your neighbours too.

Minimise the short-cropped, tidy lawn. A cut, monocultured lawn has very little value for biodiversity. Leave a few docks and thistles in the corner for the finches and leave the seed heads uncut over winter. They will be a nutritious snack for your local birds.

Some final notes

- Beware of plastic mesh! Many bird feeds, including peanuts and fat balls, are sold in plastic netting. This allows you to hang them up straight away. But don't do it. Birds become entangled in the plastic netting and can't escape. Their little legs become trapped, and they die. It's best to invest in a sturdy metal feeder, pour in the suet balls and peanuts, and dispose of the plastic mesh carefully.
- Wash the feeders. A bird feeder is like a large takeaway restaurant, and like in any restaurant, hygiene is important. Diseases such as salmonella and trichomoniasis can easily be spread by a dirty feeder. The feeders should be emptied, and washed with a brush in warm, soapy water, and it is important to wear gloves while doing this. Then change the position of the feeders, to prevent a build-up of droppings underneath.
- Big versus small birds – for when 'the large birds eat

everything, and there is nothing left for the small birds'. I love all birds, big and small, but it can be annoying when you fill a bird feeder, only to find it empty five minutes later, and a happy crow sitting nearby. To allow access to the small birds only, you can place the feeder inside an old wire dog crate, with medium sized holes. This will allow the small birds inside but keep the large ones out. Or place two mesh hanging baskets around your feeder. This will create a mesh ball, which will keep the large birds out. But remember to spare a little extra seed for the crows ...

Where to buy bird seed, bird feeders and bird boxes

- Birdwatch Ireland:
  birdwatchireland.ie/shop
- Newbawn bird seed, Wexford:
  newbawnwildbirdfeed.com
- Grow it Bio, Trim, Meath:
  info@growitbio.com
- Your local pet shop, supermarket, or hardware store.
- Nest boxes for swifts, barn owls and other birds can be bought from:
  genesisnestboxes.ie
- Your local Men's Shed group can be a great resource for bird tables and bird boxes: *menssheds.ie*

Bird activities for children

- Buy your children cheap binoculars and go on a 'twitcher' expedition, where they have to find five different types of birds.

- Buy a bird box kit. Make it, colour it and put it up.
- Join the renaissance painters and see if you can paint a goldfinch – or any other type of bird. My favourites of all bird paintings are the ones done by children of crows. Kids have the ability to capture the essence of a rook in a way no adult can.
- Make suet fat balls. Buy some lard and soften it with the heat from your hands. Get the children to crush in scraps of cheese, seeds, berries and other edible treats. Hang them in a feeder and wait for the birds. It may take a few days for the birds to try them out, but they will love them.

FLYING INSECTS

CARDER BEES

The large carder bee or moss carder bee is an incredible-looking animal. It has a big orange mane, and a hairy heart-shaped face. I know several people who look like that too, but they may not like to be compared to a bee, so they will remain nameless.

How can we tell it apart from the common carder bee? The large carder bee has blond hairs around its red mane and has blond hairs on its abdomen. The common carder bee has black hairs on its abdomen. Clearly the large carder bee prefers blondes.

This bee is in decline throughout Europe, and is listed as vulnerable on the European bee Red List. Ireland is one of its last remaining places to live, but even here, numbers are declining rapidly. And this little bee doesn't ask much from life. All it wants is a small patch of land. It is known as a doorstep forager, generally only travelling within 100 metres of its nest to feed.

An amazing man called Charles Heasman noticed that the bee was found near Skerries in Dublin, and has encouraged all the Tidy Towns groups in Fingal to help save this bee. Even Charles will admit that this little bee is fussy. It likes to nest on the ground or just underground, where it builds mossy nests, often in long grass. From 40 to 120 bees live in these nests, which last about 3 months – and crucially, their food supply must be nearby. So, ideal places for these bees include gardens with pollinating flowers all year around, hedgerows with a supply of flowers and allotments.

The plant they really adore is kidney vetch. It is to them what a good bottle of wine is to us. The kidney vetch is small and yellow, and looks woolly as it goes to seed (apparently it was used to bandage wounds in the past). It often grows on new soil or sandy areas, so you may be able to collect seeds of it while on a walk near sand dunes.

To learn more about bees and how to identify them, there are great online videos on the website of the National Biodiversity Centre – *biodiversityireland.ie*. The NBC also produce a really useful swatch – a small book that easily identifies the bees, costs very little and fits snugly in your pocket. What's not to like?

Attracting the great carder bee to your garden
- Allow dandelions, kidney vetch, bird's foot trefoil, knapweed, red clover, white clover and devil's bit scabious to grow in your garden, or in local fields. Often these flowers can be found growing alongside hedgerows. Don't cut them!
- Allow patches of long grass to grow, so that the bees can nest in peace.

Bee activities for children
- Take part in the national bumblebee survey. This involves

walking 1km once a month from March to October. The weather should be good, and you log your route and the bees you find with the National Biodiversity Centre. It is a great thing to do with kids, as they love getting good photos on mobile phones for identification later. We have spent many happy hours in family debates over whether a particular bee has hairy legs or not.

BUTTERFLIES AND MOTHS

I planted 7 acres of oats this year, for my wild birds to eat over the winter. Apparently, you can't go wrong, sowing your wild oats. I'm told they'll grow anywhere.

But alas, I had a miserable crop. Lots of thistle everywhere, and only a small amount of oats.

As I walked through my failed crop, plodding along in the field, hundreds of butterflies rose into the air. Our agricultural advisor had suggested I also plant kale, and the kale and thistle proved a winning combination for the butterflies. It was truly spectacular.

We tend to notice butterflies, but there are far more moths flying about. In fact, there are approximately 1,500 species of moths in Ireland, and only 35 species of butterfly. Identifying moths is difficult and requires skill and patience. And because we overlook moths, they can easily become extinct. We fail to notice them. If we never saw a magpie again, we would all talk about it, but who will mourn – or even notice – the passing of the hornet moth, which was last seen near Dublin, feeding on poplar trees in sunshine in 1946?

Moth species are divided into two types – micro-moths (the small ones) and macro-moths (the big guys). In the 2016 assessment of macro-moths for Ireland's Red List, the researchers looked at over half a million moth records, to see what was happening to our moth populations.

There are around 578 species of macro-moths, and the researchers looked at 501 species to decide how endangered each species was, using the International Union for Conservation of Nature (IUCN) list. If you want to be depressed, go and look at the IUCN website. As I look today, there is a cute furry mammal on their webpage, called a Cuvier's hutia. It lives in Haiti and beside the photo there is a large red arrow pointing downwards (numbers decreasing) and the designation '*endangered*'. Life in Haiti is tough for both people and wildlife.

But there is some good news. On the same page is a photo of holly, and a green line, indicating that the holly population is stable. Our Christmas wreaths are safe for the foreseeable future.

Using the IUCN Red List categories, the researchers examined our macro-moths. Forty-three species were labelled as threatened – at risk of extinction – with 7 listed as critically endangered. The IUCN defines critically endangered as being at extremely high risk of global extinction in the near future.

In total, 8% of our moths are listed as threatened, with an additional 4% listed as near-threatened or data deficient (they simply couldn't find enough moths to count). Fourteen species are regionally extinct and have not been recorded in Ireland in 50 years.

Studying moths in the wildlife world is equivalent to playing the uilleann pipes in the music world. It's difficult to learn, and you may not be popular at parties. But perhaps the difficulty is part of the magic, and the rewards are great. If you'd like to start moth watching, Moths Ireland are a wonderful bunch of people, and are really great at helping you identify moths. They must spend many hours gazing at photos sent in by amateurs like me. And when an extinction happens, they'll be the people who notice.

THE SMALL WHITE BUTTERFLY

You might see this milky-white butterfly basking in your garden, or in the countryside. Like many of us, it hates the wet, and avoids wetlands and bogs.

The males and females can be told apart from spots on their forewings. Males have one spot, while females have two. They usually have two broods a year, but often the first brood is eaten by birds, and so the second brood is more likely to survive. Strangely, the first brood has pale markings, and the second brood has darker spots.

Breeding happens from April until September. Amazingly, this tiny butterfly migrates and has been seen flying over the Irish Sea. When the male finds a lovely female, he flutters around her, releasing pheromones. It is a little like the guys in the advertisements for aftershave. And the smell seems to work. Studies using male butterflies with and without scent showed that the girls consistently chose guys who smelled. It's not all about looks with butterflies!

If the female isn't interested in the male, she will stick her abdomen high up, at 90 degrees from her body. It is known as 'tail in the air' and is a very obvious rejection of the male. Many of us have suffered this type of public rejection on dancefloors of teenage discos in the past. We can empathise with the lonely fate of the spurned male, as he makes his long trip back through the garden.

Eggs are usually laid on the underside of leaves. These butterflies are hated by gardeners as they lay their eggs on cabbages, which are then eaten by the caterpillars. To save your cabbages, cover them in horticultural fleece, and plant a few extra outside especially for the joy of watching butterflies.

Plants caterpillars love to eat include hedge mustard, annual wall rocket, garden nasturtium and turnip, and the little green caterpillar is very difficult to see as it munches through the leaves.

The caterpillar turns into a pupa, and finally the wonderful butterfly emerges. It feeds on nectar from thistles, ragwort, daisies, bluebells, common bird's foot trefoil and red clover, among other plants. A joy to have in the garden.

A YEAR IN THE LIFE OF THE BUTTERFLY

Some butterflies can have 2 or 3 generations in a year, while others can take a full year to produce one generation. Much depends on the temperature, food availability, location and species of butterfly. But you will mostly see butterflies from April to September. They can be seen feeding around flowers – amazingly, butterflies need to build up fat. A study of the North American butterfly *Eumaeus toxea* found that fatter butterflies have a higher social status than thin butterflies. They also seemed more popular with the girls, with more mating occurring with the larger lads.

The males also have a secret method of seduction. If you look at butterflies, you will see that some have black areas on their front wings. These are seduction scales – or 'androconia'. They produce pheromones, and the male drops the scales on the female, producing irresistible clouds of aphrodisiac scent, which send the females wild with passion. It's a neat trick.

Butterflies can use disguise to make themselves look scary. They are the ultimate Halloween costume designers. My father used to give me advice on dealing with dangerous situations. He said that in a fight, I should either completely underreact, and ignore everything, or overreact and act as if I was terrifying.

I'm not sure if it worked with school bullies, but it definitely works with peacock butterflies. Most of the time while resting, the peacock butterfly keeps its wings folded. The wings are dark and ragged and look like a dead leaf. And so, the butterfly plays dead. You might even brush against it, and nothing happens. But when a peacock butterfly feels threatened, you are in for a shock. The peacock butterfly has colouring which looks like eyes on the upper parts of its wings. And by rubbing its wings together it makes a *whoosh* sound – which sounds like the noise a karate expert makes while exhaling before a chop. The noise is quite loud for such a small animal, and in addition the butterfly makes an ultrasonic noise. Luckily, we can't hear this ultrasound, or we'd be terrified too.

When the butterfly is disturbed, the animal about to eat the dead leaf suddenly sees flashing eyes and hears a loud hissing noise. Needless to say, the predator runs away. Animals which are known to be frightened of peacock butterflies include blue tits, mice and chickens. Scientists think the ultrasound noises may scare bats, but are finding it difficult to devise an experiment to test this.

So, if you see a peacock butterfly – please leave it alone!

Female butterflies often lay eggs on the plant that the caterpillar will eat. It's like giving birth to your baby beside a chip van. And although the butterfly can only suck, the caterpillar can chomp. The egg stage lasts from five days to eight months, depending on the species.

Caterpillars themselves are eaten by lots of birds, and some disguise themselves by wearing camouflage. They might look like sticks or shrivelled leaves. My favourite is the comma larva, which is sometimes found on the upper side of a nettle. It looks like a bird dropping – a song thrush dropping to be precise. Who would try to eat a dropping?

Other larvae have bright colours. These colours are a message to the birds: '*Don't come near me, I'm poisonous!*'

And other caterpillars have spiky bodies. You have probably held a caterpillar and noticed this. They seem like little moving cacti. This makes the birds think twice before munching. But caterpillars and pupa can also have an enemy within. Parasites often kill them from inside their bodies.

The pupa or chrysalis is the miraculous stage. The shape of the animal completely changes. This is a dangerous time for the animal, as it can't move and is effectively trapped while changing shape. Just like ourselves when we sign up for a gym membership! But most pupa are really well camouflaged – in fact some butterfly pupae have never been seen by humans. The pupa stage can last from two weeks to nine months. And our blue butterflies have devised an ingenious method of protection. The pupa (and larva) of the holly blue butterfly appear to use bodyguards. They sing to ants by making noises within their pupa, and then feed them a sweet, nectar-like liquid. It is thought that the ants may protect them in return. In the mysterious web of life, many species seem interwoven with other species, and we still don't always know why.

GARDENING FOR BUTTERFLIES

The god of Irish butterflies is a man called Jesmond Harding. He is a fascinating person and his book, *The Irish Butterfly Book*, is essential reading. He also has really interesting talks on gardening for butterflies on YouTube.

To attract butterflies, try to have lots of different habitats in your garden. Flower borders with *Hebe*, English lavender and *Buddleja davidii* will provide lots of nectar, but remember that native species are best, so a wildflower meadow is really wonderful. Try to add some wet area, with a pond and a woodland/hedgerow effect with grey willow, common hazel and guilder rose.

A rockery is a great place for butterflies, as they often bask on stones. Then add some ox-eye daisies, bloody cranesbill or kidney vetch. I often speak to graveyard restoration groups about the importance of these areas to butterflies. The big headstones are ideal basking spaces for butterflies, and they need to be encouraged to plant areas for butterflies and leave some untidy areas with nettles for the caterpillars.

Jesmond also recommends watering plants in hot weather, as this improves nectar release. Bare soil can also be sprayed with water, to allow butterflies to drink the dissolved salts.

And remember the caterpillars! Leave an area of nettles in the garden, and throw away the pesticides.

GARDENING FOR INSECTS

The All-Ireland Pollinator Plan (*pollinators.ie*) is a fantastic initiative, which encourages us all to improve our local areas for pollinating insects. It includes ideas for gardens, farms, local communities, businesses, transport corridors, sports clubs, golf courses, windfarms, group water schemes and faith communities. Booklets are available free of charge on their website, and are accompanied by how-to guides and lists of pollinator-friendly plants to get you started.

Some ideas to start with

• Reduce the amount of mowing in your garden. I put two bat detectors on a field in Dublin, 500 metres from each other. One area was cut short, and one was left as long grass. The grass was just ordinary ryegrass, with no wildflowers. But the bat activity over the long grass was four times the level of the bat activity over the cut grass. And why were the bats were enjoying the long grass so much more? They were munching away on insects. Even long grass with a poor species mix has a lot more insects than short grass.

So cut paths through your garden, instead of cutting the entire garden – and print off some lovely posters from the All-Ireland Pollinator Plan. A pretty poster on a stick will let everyone know that you are not sinking into squalor, but instead are doing your bit to protect nature.

Let the dandelions and clover grow, and the flowers will provide fantastic amounts of nectar for bees. If you have a bumper dandelion crop, you can make dandelion syrup. I'm lucky to have a wonderful next-door neighbour who treats me to a pot of this syrup every year. It is liquid gold – I can understand why the bees like dandelions so much.

- Get rid of pesticides. Otherwise, you will be killing the animal you wish to protect. It may be better for your human health too.

- Plant hanging baskets and window boxes with pollinator-friendly herbs, such as chives, rosemary and thyme. Both you and the bees will then have a local food supply. The All-Ireland Pollinator Plan also has advice on other suitable plants for window boxes.

- Plant bulbs for pollinators, such as crocus and snowdrops. Sadly, daffodils and tulips are not good for pollinators. As a general guide, single flowers are usually better than plants with double flower heads, and perennials are usually better than annuals.

- Provide shelter with deadwood, insect boxes, bundles of old raspberry canes, etc, and provide a few areas along the banks of your garden that have bare soil. We had bees nesting in a hole in a bank near our house – until a badger arrived, dug them out and ate them!

- Think in three dimensions. What can you do to increase the height in your garden? Can you plant trees or hedge-row? Can you plant ivy along walls? What about using window boxes? Try to green areas that were previously grey concrete.

A WORD ABOUT NEONICOTINOIDS, OR ❧NEONICS❧

These pesticides were invented in 1991. They are systemic, which means that the plant soaks up the pesticide and it is found within the plant, as opposed to a pesticide that sits directly on the leaves. Neonic pesticides are absorbed – so all parts of the plant contain it, including the flowers and leaves.

Many seeds are coated with it, or it can be applied as a soil drench or sprayed onto crops.

In 2014, the Global Task Force on Systemic Pesticides looked at 1,121 scientific papers and concluded that neonics were causing significant damage to a wide range of beneficial invertebrate species, and were a key factor in the decline of bees. They also put birds and reptiles at risk, and have an effect on microbes, fish and amphibians.

The problem is that neonics can persist in the soil for months and years, and when they break down, their com-pounds (metabolites of neonics) can become even more toxic. The report says that some neonics are at least 5,000 to 10,000 times more toxic than DDT.

They are nerve poisons and alter the tunnelling behaviour in earthworms that try to carry them away. In other insects they seem to impair memory, taste and smell, and they reduce foraging in bees.

To make things worse, these pesticides can contaminate nearby wild features, such as hedgerows and rivers.

So, get them out of your garden shed! (Dispose of them carefully!)

THE BIG PICTURE – AND WHAT YOU CAN DO ABOUT IT

Issues such as climate change and air, light and water pollution affect animals as well as people. In many cases, we have only recently discovered the dangers of pollution to human health, and we have yet to discover the effects on animal health. Good air and water are crucial to all life forms. They are the basic building blocks of biodiversity. There is no point in planting hanging baskets for pollinators while the local air and water turn grey. It's like spending money on high fashion while your skeleton crumbles. When I talk to Tidy Towns groups, I often ask them to check their local water for pollutants or walk around their towns with a cheap air quality monitor. They are shocked at the results.

CLIMATE CHANGE

We all know that climate change is a huge problem. The problem is so huge, it makes us want to run away screaming 'we're all going to die!', or stick our heads in the sand and hope the problem somehow sorts itself out. It won't.

As with the biodiversity crisis, there are small actions you can take to reduce your carbon footprint. Many are easy to do, and will even save you money.

What are the greenhouse gasses?

- Carbon dioxide: Once carbon dioxide heads into the atmosphere, it hangs around there for hundreds of years, like an unwelcome ghost. Most of our carbon dioxide release is caused by burning fossil fuels and the manufacture of cement. I start shouting at the television whenever I see a supposed 'eco-house' with cement floors, walls and worktops.

  To capture carbon, we need to plant trees – but then burning these trees or allowing them to rot just releases the embedded carbon back into the atmosphere. We need to use wood in our homes and in industry as a carbon store. Other carbon storage heroes include phytoplankton in the sea, and of course bogland, which stores enormous amounts.

- Methane: This gas has caused 30–50% of the global warming temperature increase. It is highly potent, with a stronger effect than carbon dioxide at lower concentrations. But the good news is that it doesn't last as long in the atmosphere. If we could stop methane emissions today, the concentration of methane in the atmosphere would be halved in just 10 years. And in another ten years, that concentration would be halved again.

  Methane is released by the production of natural gas, by agriculture (cows belching), rotting in landfills, biomass combustion and rice production. Natural methane sinks include the atmosphere itself and soil.

- Nitrous oxide: This is also known as laughing gas, but really it should make us cry. The nitrogen gases (NOx) and the gangs they hang around in are bad news. They are the bogey men of gases. Nitrous oxide is 300 times more potent than carbon dioxide and hangs around in the atmosphere for ages (approximately 114 years). Three-quarters of the emissions of this gas come from agriculture.
- Ozone: Like all of us, ozone can be both good and bad. When it is high in the atmosphere, it is good, forming a layer that blocks UV light. At lower levels, it is harmful to human health.

WHAT CAN I DO?

- Switch your electricity account to a 100% renewable energy provider. This will instantly cut your carbon footprint. Websites such as *bonkers.ie* make it easy to switch energy providers.
- Change your pension to an ethical one, which does not invest in oil and gas fields. This might also save you money in the long run. If we were to use all of the fuel in our current oil and gas fields, we would tip the planet into a climate meltdown. Simply put, we cannot use the oil and gas in these reserves. These fossil fuel reserves will therefore become stranded assets – something that cannot make a viable economic return. If we use them, and they make a profit, it will cost us the planet. So, get your personal money out of them immediately.
- If you are in a group pension scheme with your company, question the ethics of the pension. I know of doctors and

nurses who have joined forces asking for their pensions to be divested from fossil fuels because of the human health implications (smog) of burning fossil fuels. And Ireland has become the first country to divest from fossil fuels. The Irish Strategic Investment Fund, which manages over eight billion euros in assets and is run by the NTMA, has sold off its investments in fossil fuel companies. Ireland leads the way!

- Insulate your house. Many libraries have kits they will lend you to help you find where heat leaks from your house. Often it is through the attic, or at draughty areas around ill-fitting windows. I live in an old house, and the fight against draughts and cold is constant. If you can afford to upgrade your insulation (and this should be on everyone's bucket list), look at the grants offered by the Sustainable Energy Authority of Ireland (SEAI). The grants can be higher for people on low incomes.
- Eat less meat and dairy. Try some of the vegetarian alternatives to mince, sausages and burgers. I bet you won't be able to tell the difference. The oat and soya milks are lovely too. And they're better for your cholesterol levels.
- Look at your transport. Can you use a bus or train? What about a bike or electric bike? Can you take less flights? What about investing in an electric car? Electric cars cost a lot to purchase, but they save a lot of money in running costs.
- Use wood everywhere – in your buildings and in furniture. You are capturing and storing carbon within your home.
- Join Friends of the Earth, Voice, An Taisce, Trócaire or Stop Climate Chaos, to lobby and work for a better world.

- Consume less. I recently read a study on pigs. Pigs are highly intelligent and love novelty. Sometimes they like toys, even bad toys, simply because they are new (my pet pigs think the best toy you can get is a bale of straw). I reckon I'm a bit like a pig. Sometimes I want something new, even though I already have a wardrobe full of clothes and more books than I can cram into my home. When I feel like a shopping spree, I buy in second-hand shops. A win for the environment, the charity running the shop and my pocket.

AIR POLLUTION

I spent many years working in cardiology in hospitals in Dublin in the 1980s and 1990s. Patients would regularly arrive at the hospital having heart attacks. In fact, one in three of us will probably die from heart or lung disease. We thought that the causes of heart attacks were smoking, poor diets, genetics and lack of exercise. We never thought that breathing poor-quality air could be an issue.

But when Minister Mary Harney brought in a smoky coal ban in the 1990s, cardiac deaths in Dublin dropped by 15%. Deaths from lung disease dropped by 10%, and deaths from everything else (except trauma) dropped by 7%. But what if you lived outside Dublin? I lobbied relentlessly for cleaner air, and was lucky to meet Minister Phil Hogan, who took an interest in air quality. Health and environmental groups were lobbying hard for improvements in our air, yet in 2013, approximately 3,400 people died prematurely in Ireland from poor air quality. You may have known some of them – sadly, I knew several.

Minister Hogan extended the smoky coal ban to towns with over 15,000 residents. By 2016, there were 1,180 premature deaths per year caused by poor air quality. And in 2020, Minister Eamon Ryan extended the ban on smoky coal to towns with a population of over 10,000 people. You may not have voted for these politicians. You may not like them. But their good political decisions may have saved your life.

Unfortunately, we can't see the danger in small particles of smoke. We might avoid fast cars and people who look dangerous, but we imagine that the air in our living rooms and on our streets is safe. In fact, we don't even think about it. But this invisible killer is in our midst.

THE MAIN AIR POLLUTANTS ARE:

- Nitrogen monoxide and dioxide: These are produced by diesel engines in cars, aeroplanes and gas-burning boilers. Ireland has exceeded the EU emission limits for these gases since 2010.
- Ammonia: This comes from agriculture – fertiliser spreading, slurry, urine and poultry manure. The amount of ammonia measured in our air rises every year and now exceeds our EU emissions limits.
- Ozone: Ozone is produced by the sun when it hits organic matter when nitrogen dioxide is about. A study with the title 'Every Breath You Take' showed that 97% of European citizens are exposed to ground ozone levels above those deemed safe by the World Health Organisation. It's enough to make you gasp.
- Non-methane Volatile Organic Matter: This dust come from

a variety of sources, including from forests. Although some VOCs can be problematic in themselves, the main trouble occurs when they meet up with nitrogen and form ozone. They are in many household products, such as paints, glues and even your sofa.

- Particulate matter: This can be particles of anything, and as a general rule, the smaller the particle, the more dangerous it is. Particles can be so small, they can cross happily into your bloodstream and lungs, and give you a heart attack. There has been a lot of research on PM2.5, particles of less than 2.5 micrometres in size. These are very, very small pieces of dust. A human hair is 70 micrometres thick, and difficult to see, so we can only imagine what size PM2.5 is. As in all good thrillers, you will never see your silent killer. PM2.5 release is caused by burning wood, coal and oil.

WHAT CAN I DO?

- Stop burning wood, coal and oil. Switch your heating to electric sources. I recently bought a cheap air pollution monitor. I was horrified when I placed it by my wood-burning stove – all the dials on the monitor immediately turned to red, indicating severe pollution. I am gassing my family within my living room. Electric heating is cleaner, but can be expensive. In an ideal world, people should be financially supported to change their heating systems.
- Plant trees, hedgerow, gardens, green walls and green roofs. Plants absorb many of the contaminants in air pollution and are really important for pollution control within cities. In cities such as Copenhagen and Zurich, building regulations

state that all new buildings must have green roofs. These fight air pollution, provide areas for wildlife and insulate homes. The most dramatic green buildings in Europe are the Bosco Verticale, a pair of forest-covered skyscrapers in Milan, Italy. Have a look at them on Google – you will want to live there.

- Plants also help with indoor air quality, so a few houseplants will act as a cheap air filtration system for your home. All they ask for in return is a small amount of watering.

- Switch from diesel cars to another form of transport. Diesel cars emit a lot of pollutants, and the passengers in these cars fail to notice that they are sitting in a lethal smog. When I see a mother strapping her newborn into a diesel car, I feel the urge to stop her (though I stopped being quite so judgemental when I realised I was smothering my own children with our wood fire at home).

- If you must drive, electric cars are best – once they are fuelled with renewable energy. Otherwise, you are just creating the smog in another place.

- Buy second-hand furniture. I'm a great fan of second-hand sofas, largely because they are cheap to buy. I have three in my house. And sofas release most VOCs at the start of their lives. By buying second hand, the VOCs have already been released in someone else's home, and your home will be safer.

- Stop idling your car. Switch it off while you are waiting. And ask the school bus at the local school to switch off their engine too. They are suffocating your children.

WATER POLLUTION

When my daughter was just over one year old, she became really ill, and ended up in hospital for several nights. It seems that the cause may have been cryptosporidium, caused by contaminated drinking water. She was very tiny and very, very sick.

Water pollution is a huge problem in Ireland – our rivers, lakes, bathing and ground water look fine to the naked eye, and people may baulk at the idea of spending millions of taxpayers' money on water treatment plants and better sewage systems. But clean water is essential to our health.

You can look at the data on your local river on the website of the Environmental Protection Agency. But it's always more fun to do a water quality check yourself.

Inland Fisheries Ireland produce a Water Pollution Indicator. It is a large fold-out guide to the animals living in your local river. Firstly, you must wade into a river and kick around. We have done this with local schoolchildren, and they are amazed that a school day can be spent paddling. And that you can grow up to be an ecologist and do this for a living.

The paddling will move the silt around – then you must catch the creatures you find in the mud. The little animals are carefully transferred via a net to a bucket of water on the bank, where you can study them closely. And the animals themselves will let you know whether the water is clean or polluted.

After counting the creatures, you can return them safely to the stream. The guide from Inland Fisheries will introduce you to the animals.

The stonefly will only live in unpolluted waters. Having a stonefly in your river is like having John Bonham from Led

Zeppelin in your house. Stoneflies use the magic of drumming to attract mates. The male starts banging its belly and listens for a female nearby. The female will listen out for the drummer and make her choice. Will she go for Animal from 'The Muppets'? Or perhaps Phil Collins is more her style? Drummers throughout the world should champion pristine water quality, because this drumming for love can only happen beside good quality waters. Without stoneflies, our rivers will be quieter and less musical places.

If your water is imperfect, but still pretty good, you can find dragonfly nymphs. A great thing about dragonflies is that they allow us to assess the water quality without even getting our feet wet. Just sit on the bank and look for dragonflies. They are so big, you can't miss them. The nymphs stay in the water for up to two years before they turn into dragonflies, and they can't swim. They propel themselves in an amazing way: They pull water into their rectum, and with a large splat, they propel themselves using jet propulsion from their bums. I think some of my children have tried this method in the past. They also have gills in their rectums and can filter air. A whole new approach to talking through your backside.

As we move to streams with more water pollution, we will still find the mayfly (*Caenis*). This type of mayfly has earned the name 'the angler's curse', as it is really delicious to fish, and if it is around the fish will chase it, ignoring all other juicy morsels temptingly placed on hooks.

As you get to more polluted waters, the names of the animals get worse. How about the hog louse, or leech? The bloodworm, the bladder snail. Or my favourite, the rat-tailed maggot. This is an odd-looking creature that can survive in the worst of waters. It has a long tube at the base of its body, which looks like a rat's tail (though much smaller). This tube is a type of periscope, allowing the creature to breath in murky waters. This ugly-looking creature does, however, have its moment of glory, when it turns from a ratty maggot into a fabulous hoverfly. A real-life ugly duckling story.

What can I do?

- Protect your stream from silt and pollutants by planting natural barriers of hedgerows nearby. They will slow down, and may prevent, effluent from entering the watercourse.
- Keep farm animals away from watercourses. Grants are available to farmers for fencing watercourses. Pasture pumps or solar drinking pumps can be used as drinkers.
- Report pollution issues to the EPA and Inland Fisheries Ireland.
- Clean out your septic tank regularly and check that it works properly.
- Take part in Water Quality Citizen Science projects, such as Water Blitz.
- Where is your wastewater being treated? Lobby councils and politicians to improve our wastewater treatment.

WHAT TO DO IF YOU FIND A SICK ANIMAL

Often it is best to do nothing. Many fledglings have a few wobbly days on the ground, when they can't fly properly and are being fed by their parents. Leave them alone. Their parents will look after them.

Some animals hide their young in grass. The mums keep away from the young, trying not to attract attention to them. But well-meaning people find seemingly 'abandoned' fawns each year in the Phoenix Park and are keen to look after them. Again, it is best to leave them alone.

Baby bats tend to get lost in midsummer and enter houses. They can be scooped up in a box and tipped outside on an upstairs windowsill for their mums to collect.

With all young animals, their parents' care is a million times better than anything you can do. But sometimes the parents are killed, or the young animal is in a dangerous place or is injured. What should you do?

Firstly, remember that the animal is wild. It is sore, panicked and afraid of you. When you go to catch it, the animal expects to be eaten. It will bite, scratch or peck, and do all it can to escape. It is important to take care of yourself. Use gloves where needed, and get help from experienced wildlife rescuers. They will have specialised catching poles and protective equipment.

For most sick or injured animals, warmth, darkness and water are the best things you can provide. You will need to bring the animal to a vet for assessment. If you find a sick animal, email Kildare Wildlife Rescue at *info@kwr.ie* with a photograph or short video, your name, location and phone number, and they will put you in touch with your nearest rehabber.

Wildlife Rehabilitation Ireland provides internet advice on first aid for individual animals at *irishwildlifematters.ie*. They plan to build a wildlife hospital, and it will be a wonderful place. Throughout the country, there are specialist rehabbers –

Kildare Wildlife Rescue, Bat Rehabilitation Ireland, the Irish Seal Sanctuary, Hedgehog Rescue Dublin, the Hogsprickle Wildlife Carers and Ireland's Wildlife Rehabilitators Association, for example.

These kind-hearted and unpaid volunteers spend their hours caring for wildlife, and with any spare time, raise funds for animal medicines and vets' bills. If you bring an animal to them, please also try to give them a donation, a box of chocolates and a large hug. They are amazing people.

BUILD YOUR OWN POND

If you're only going to do one thing for nature, build a pond. It is the easiest way to get the largest amount of wildlife into a garden. However, this part of the book must come with a health warning: Building ponds is very addictive. One pond will never be enough, and soon your garden will become a ribbon of ponds, marsh and wetland areas, as you become more experimental in pond design. For a lazy gardener like me, a garden pond can become a spectacular feature, requiring little or no maintenance. Nothing beats sitting beside some water, watching the world go by.

The first pond we built on our farm was in the basin of a field. It's always good to put the pond in a low-lying area, where water naturally collects. Our pond-building technique involved handing some money to a neighbour with a digger and instructing him to 'go crazy'. There may be better approaches, but this worked well for us, and there was much excitement when our neighbour asked if we wanted an island. We were now joining the league of the rich and famous, just like Richard Branson and Charlie Haughey, with our very own island.

We danced around the kitchen, singing as many island

songs as possible – Joe Dolan would have been proud of us – and told our neighbour that yes, we really wanted an island.

Half an hour later, we were the proud owners of Pudding Island, a ball of black mud about the size of a kitchen table, which looks strangely like a Christmas pudding. Pudding Island is separated from the rest of the field by a moat of 3 metres of water.

Our island is solid, but it is possible to build floating islands, like little rafts with vegetation on top. They can be large or small, and built of anything that floats – inverted plastic buckets, PVC pipes or bits of wood. Islands are great – they provide small, secluded places for wildlife, and protection from predators. Most importantly, they provide additional edges to ponds – and pond edges are the most important places for wildlife. An ideal pond will have lots of edges. Instead of the traditional circular pond, it could be a figure-of-eight, half-moon or starfish shape.

The pond edges should be sloped with a gradient of 1 in 5. Shallow water in ponds is better for wildlife than deep water, and having a long, shallow area of pond makes it very safe. Children, adults and hedgehogs are likely to step back from cold, marshy and shallow water.

How do you keep the water in? This seems a strange problem in Ireland, where water appears to arrive in an endless supply. The first step is to look at your farm or garden. Is there somewhere that water naturally collects? Or look at a nearby stream in summertime. At what level is the water? The level of the stream will show you the water table, and how deep you will need to dig to get below it to have an endless supply of groundwater.

You could use pond liner. It is expensive, and obviously it is plastic, but it works well. Protect your investment in expensive pond liner by making sure that all sharp stones are removed from the base of your pond pit. You might like to add sand or compact the soil to make a soft area for the pond liner to rest on. Pond liner should be fitted gently, as stretching will damage it. Sunlight can also degrade the liner, so at the pond edges, put stones over it.

Another way of holding water is by using Bentonite clay as a pond liner. This has the added advantage of being a natural product, and it seems to have amazing properties – you can even use it to clean your hair.

When you have your liner in place, add soil to the base of your pond, and wait for the animals and plants to arrive. In theory, you should wait for them to arrive naturally, and you should avoid large plants such as bulrushes, which will quickly take over. But a pond of bulrushes is such a lovely place. Our first pond has been taken over by bulrushes and dragonflies, and it is wonderful. And we can always build another pond!

I occasionally suffer from pond envy. One of the best ponds I've ever seen has been built by a family in north County Dublin. Rainwater is collected from the roof of the house and pumped into the pond, which has a deeper section in the middle where you can swim. It is simply amazing. The edges are shallow and have a fabulous collection of plants, and the middle is the best swimming pool I've ever seen. If I was in government and allowed to pass odd laws, my pond law would insist that every gym and sports club must divert their roof water to one of these ponds. Imagine the joy of swimming with frogs, instead of swimming with chlorinated water and plastic toys in the local indoor swimming pool.

Ponds don't have to be large to be effective. Many animals, such as bees, only have a small territory. If there is nowhere for them to drink, an otherwise perfect area is useless to them. The Drimnagh Community Environmental Group in Dublin have an amazing plan. They asked a local florist for their waste flower buckets, and set about creating mini-ponds in their area. In their workshops, they give advice, a bucket and some native oxygenating plants. And off you go! Putting in a bucket pond takes less than an hour, and hey presto, you have a mini-pond. Bucket ponds can go anywhere, and are perfect for small gardens or balconies. The addition of stones to the bucket gives you mini-islands, and an escape route for any small animals or insects that may fall in. Like a small aquarium, an outdoor bucket pond will become a tiny ecosystem of its own. The environmental group in Drimnagh is really amazing – there are now over 150 ponds in place in their area. Their project shows what can be achieved in urban housing estates, with waste buckets and enthusiasm.

Now it's time to put this book down and start digging. You will feel like a millionaire if you own an island. In fact, you will feel like a millionaire if you simply have a pond. So, treat yourself. Everyone deserves a pond (or two) of their own!

FROGS

The common frog is found all over Ireland, but its numbers are declining throughout Europe. It is thought that one factor causing trouble for frogs is the increase in ultraviolet light, which damages their skin.

Frogs eat slugs, flies and earth-worms. I have often found them hiding in horse manure, waiting for unsuspecting insects to land.

A YEAR IN THE LIFE OF A FROG

Male frogs find a pond and croak loudly to attract a female. The female frog is larger and rather slippery, so mating is a challenge for the male. He needs to cling on and fertilise the eggs as the female releases them. As Kermit has rightly said, 'It's not easy being green.' To solve this problem, males have a sticky patch on their fingers, called a nuptial patch, which helps them hold on to a slippery female. Scientists have recently found that a special protein is released from these patches around mating time. It is called amplexin, and no-one really knows what its function is, but salamanders release something similar when they are in the throes of passion, so it must enhance their sexual gymnastics.

The female frog can release up to 4,000 eggs, and the jelly around the spawn insulates it against cold weather. Spawn clumps together to further help insulate it.

The tadpoles hatch, and over ten weeks, the magic of metamorphosis occurs, with back legs growing, then front legs, then bulging eyes appearing. It is fascinating to watch. Finally the tail disappears – and hey presto, it's a frog!

Only one in 10,000 tadpoles makes it to adulthood, and it can be 2 to 3 years before they breed. But frogs can then live for 10 to 15 years. Frogs live on land, returning to the water to breed.

Attracting frogs to your area

- Build ponds – the ideal wildlife pond has different depths, with ledges. It is important that the pond is sloped, so frogs can get in and out. And if you only have a small garden, don't despair – a friend of mine has a small basin the size of a sink buried in her garden, and it is used by frogs. It needs to be topped up regularly with water, but is very successful.
- Frogs like still water, so don't put waterfalls or fountains in your pond.
- Keep your pond free of chemicals, and don't introduce fish.
- Allow some dead matter and untidiness. The tadpoles will eat it and shelter under it.
- Frogs need shelter. Long grass, clay pots on their sides, rocks and woodpiles are great. Our frogs and newts love to rest within the plastic folds of old wellies and waders. Our pond looks as if Imelda Markos has visited and dumped a strange shoe collection.
- Join the Herpetological Society of Ireland.
- Keep dogs and cats away from froggy areas to keep disturbance to a minimum.

Activities for Children

- Take part in the 'Hop To It' frog survey, undertaken by the Irish Peatland Conservation Council.

MAKE YOUR COMMUNITY A NATURE RESERVE

opefully by this stage in the book, you will have ivy falling over your apartment balcony, long grass in the garden of your house or a new pond in your farm. But what of the wider community? Small pockets of biodiversity are wonderful, but can just be islands unless we connect them together. And connecting biodiverse areas can be easy to do.

HEDGEROWS

Have a look at the hedges in your area. Is there any way they can be connected? Are there railings or patches of grass that could have hedgerow planted alongside?

It is important to see what each area is used for. If there are young children who like to play in a patch of grass on a housing estate, plant clumps of hedges and trees that will regrow if broken by a stray football. In areas with groups of elderly people, I have planted heritage apple trees and fruiting hedges – blackcurrants, redcurrants, gooseberries and blackberries. This creates a 'Food for Free' trail for people and birds, and it is lovely to spend a day picking blackberries with the grandchildren before making a pie.

Safety and security might be an issue when choosing a hedge. People might be wary of hedgerow against their house wall. A prickly hedgerow such as blackthorn, whitethorn or holly will provide an added level of security to the homeowner.

Ideally, hedges should be thick, high in places, dotted with trees and connected to each other.

TREES

There is a tree for every area. Small trees such as rowan can be planted almost anywhere. Have a look at a map of your area and see which areas lack trees. Speak to the local residents. Tell them about the benefits of trees – they cut down on the air pollution in the area and will increase the value of their property. Trees can also be used to screen light pollution.

Sadly, scientists have mapped out the 'Luxury Effect'. Researchers plotted biodiversity maps on top of maps showing people's income levels. The rich have more of everything, including more biodiversity. Their streets tend to have more mature trees, and they have larger gardens. Because of this, it is important to ensure that lower-income areas of the community have special attention paid to their local biodiversity. People on low incomes suffer more from air pollution, and can also suffer more from stress. Being around trees lowers your stress levels. Many countries practise 'forest bathing'. It is a wonderful idea, involving sitting or walking near trees. The trees release natural chemicals, and this forest aromatherapy works by calming us. And it's cheaper than a day in a health spa.

Japanese researchers lead the way on forest bathing. They sent some people into the forest, and others on a tourist city break. Then they asked them to pee into a jar, to measure their stress levels. Those who went to the forest had a significant decrease in adrenaline and noradrenalin – our stress hormones. Walks in the forest are routinely prescribed in Japan, and every health centre and hospital in Ireland should have an area where you can sit by a tree. Because now we know why all the tree huggers are so zen!

As a general rule, trees should have a range of heights, and be mostly native. And trees should have an understory – long grass, plants and scrub around their base.

Dead wood is also important. If a tree must be felled for safety reasons, ask if it can be pollarded and left in place. Beetles and a range of insects, fungi, lichens and mosses love to live in deadwood habitat. It is a natural insect hotel. So leave dead wood and fallen branches on the ground.

WATERWAYS

Streams, rivers and lakes are major commuting routes for many animals. It is essential that no light pollution falls onto them. Many humans enjoy being in the spotlight, being noticed and getting attention, but if you are a nocturnal animal in the spotlight, your predators know where to find you. Many film stars and other famous people have also been eaten alive by the media when their limelight became too intense. Darkness is wonderful camouflage.

As many pollutants come from the land, an ideal way to stop them is by making a natural barrier between land and water. This can be achieved by leaving strips of long grass, or by planting trees and hedgerows. The area by a river may become damp or flooded, so if you are planting near waterways, use plants that are tolerant of wetness, such as alder and willow.

If you see anywhere an animal can be trapped, make an escape route. I have seen animals drown in upturned buckets, water buttes, cattle troughs and under cattle grids. A ramp made of wood will allow an animal to escape.

CHILDREN AND NATURE

Nature should be part of our daily lives. It should not be locked away, like something foreign and distant. And children need to experience nature on a daily basis. I start ranting whenever I see housing estates with blank green grass areas – monocultures of ryegrass with nothing interesting for children to see or do.

Kids might like to play football – and will follow the football onto a road without thinking if it shoots off the grass. A hedgerow along the side of the road can prevent this. And children should be encouraged to play with nature. Dead, fallen tree trunks are places to sit and to climb. Willow huts and mazes are really easy to grow, and they regrow easily if broken. Little clumps of trees provide places for hide and seek. Trees such as hazel will also regrow if damaged. And plant a few horse chestnut trees. I still feel the magic of opening the prickly outside of a horse chestnut seed to reveal the wonder of a conker within.

Conkers can be strung on string and used to bash other

conkers. Or they can make fabulous play animals when holes are drilled into them and matchstick legs are inserted, with little conker animal heads and bodies.

USING THE LAW

The law is easier to use than you might imagine. In many cases, you just need to report the problem, and someone else will enforce it.

WILDLIFE CRIME

If someone is hunting on your land without your permission; or if you suspect a poisoning of a bird; cutting of a hedgerow in the nesting season; bat roost destruction; or any other wildlife issue – Call NPWS on 01 8882000 or email *natureconservation@housing.gov.ie*. They will put you in touch with your local ranger.

WATER POLLUTION

Call Inland Fisheries Ireland on 0818 347424.

LITTERING

There is a 'See It, Say It' app that you can download to your phone, and easily photograph a problem that can be logged with your local authority.

OTHER INCIDENCES

Call the Gardaí on 999 or 112. There is talk of a specialised unit of the Gardaí being set up to deal with crime against animals. This would be really helpful. We will wait and see.

FURTHER HELP

Wildlife Crime Ireland are a voluntary organisation and have lots of information on how to record a crime, and what to do next. They work with PAW Ireland, who have developed an app that you can download onto your phone to help report crimes. Their website is *wildlifecrime.ie*.

WHAT'S GOING ON? THE AARHUS CONVENTION

Sometimes it can be difficult to know where to start. Is your next-door neighbour really planning to set up a nuclear power plant or are you just imagining it? The Aarhus Convention is your friend in this scenario and will let you know what is really happening. It was adopted by the United Nations in 1998, and there are three main parts which will be helpful to you:

ACCESS TO INFORMATION

You have the right to access information on the environment that is held by public bodies.

This includes county councils (for planning permissions), the EPA, the NPWS and in fact any public body. The information can also include information on public health where it is related to the environment, and information on plans and policies. Now you can find out if your neighbour has applied for planning permission, and if government policy supports the development of local nuclear power plants.

To get this information, send an Access to Information on the Environment request (an AIE) to whoever holds the information. They must reply to you within a month.

ENVIRONMENTAL DECISION-MAKING

You have the right to participate in environmental decision-making.

The key word here is participate. You cannot be simply consulted and fobbed off. You will see many government consultations online, and a really important way to make a difference is by spending long and tedious hours filling in these consultations and being an advocate for nature. This is vitally important work, and I plan to do lots of it when I am aged and living in a nursing home.

Take a look at plans and policies by councils, government and other public bodies. And have your say.

ACCESS TO JUSTICE

You have a right to challenge decisions.

What happens when we hit a problem? Suppose we are not given the information we need, or are denied participation in decision making? The third part of the convention deals with access to justice. Taking granny's advice of 'never going to bed on a row', the convention insists on 'fair, equitable and timely' procedures, and the costs of making up must not be 'prohibitively expensive'. This means that the problem should be sorted out quickly, and it should not cost too much to go to court.

EUROPEAN LAW

Irish law is really confusing, so when you want to know if something is legal or illegal, I would suggest you look at European law. European law is written in a way that is very easy to understand. The main laws involving wildlife are the Habitats Directive, the Birds Directive and the EIA Directive. And if Ireland is breaking these laws, you can take a case to Europe.

I have tried this myself, when I noticed that the Irish Wildlife Act was written in a way that made taking prosecutions impossible. And there was no monitoring of our rare species. I didn't know how to contact the Commission, so I attended a meeting with the European Commissioner for the Environment. Her name was Margot Wallström and she was surrounded by many important people. I realised at the meeting that I was never going to get to talk to her, so I found her handbag and slipped a letter inside. The letter told of our issues with the protection of wildlife. Her team called me two days later, and five years later, we won our case in court.

Going to the European Courts is a slow process, so always try sorting out problems using the Irish justice system first.

If all else fails and you need Europe, the Commission switchboard's phone number is (+32) 2 29911 (ask for DG Environment), and their address is:

Directorate-General for Environment.

European Commission 1049 Brussel, Belgium.

It might prevent you from fiddling with the handbags of European Environmental Commissioners.

LAWS PROTECTING IRISH WILDLIFE

(The boring part of the book. Only read this part in an emergency.)

Below is a list of some of the legal protection for Irish species and habitats. Don't bother reading it now, but it's good to quote this stuff if you are trying to prevent damage to wildlife.

BIRD PROTECTION

The Wildlife (Amendment) Act (2000), The EU Birds Directive, The EU Habitats Directive. SPAs under Directive 2009/147/EC. Statutory Instrument 94/119, SI 233/1998 and SI 378/2005. European Birds and Natural Habitats Regulations 2011.

BAT PROTECTION

Bats are protected under the 1996 Wildlife Act, the 2000 Wildlife (Amendment) Act, Stat Ist 94 of 1997, Stat Ist 378 of 2005, The Habitats Directive, The Bonn and Bern Conventions and the Euro bats agreement. The European Community (Natural Habitats) Regulations S.I. No 94 of 1997 states:

23(1) The minister shall take the requisite measures to establish a system of strict protection for the fauna consisting of the animal species set out in Part 1 of the First Schedule prohibiting –

(a) All forms of deliberate capture or killing of specimens of those species in the wild.

(b) The deterioration or destruction of breeding sites or resting places of those species.

The EU Habitats Directive Article 12(1) of the Council

Directive 92/43/EEC on the conservation of natural habitats and wild fauna and flora (Habitats Directive) states:

Member States shall take the requisite measures to establish a system of strict protection for the animal species listed in Annex IV(a) and their natural range, prohibiting:

(a) all forms of deliberate capture or killing of specimens of these species in the wild.

(b) deliberate disturbance of these species, particularly during the period of breeding, rearing, hibernation, and migration.

(c) deliberate destruction or taking of eggs from the wild.

(d) deterioration or destruction of breeding sites or resting places.

The EU Habitats Directive (92/43/EEC) lists all Irish bat species in Annex IV and one Irish species, the lesser horseshoe bat (*Rhinolophus hipposideros*), in Annex II. Annex II includes animal and plant species of community interest whose conservation requires the designation of Special Areas of Conservation (SACs) because they are endangered, rare, vulnerable or endemic. Annex IV includes various species that require strict protection. Article 11 of the Habitats Directive requires member states to monitor all species listed in the Habitats Directive, and Article 17 requires states to report to the EU on the findings of monitoring schemes.

The Bern and Bonn Conventions: Ireland is also a signatory to several conservation agreements pertaining to bats, such as the Bern and Bonn Conventions. The European Bats Agreement (EUROBATS) is an agreement under the Bonn Convention. Ireland and the UK are 2 of the 31 signatories. The Agreement includes an Action Plan, with priorities for implementation. Devising strategies for monitoring of populations of selected bat species in Europe is among the resolutions of EUROBATS.

Article 6 of the Bern Convention, or the 'Convention on the Conservation of European Wildlife and Natural Habitats', states:

Each Contracting Party shall take appropriate and necessary legislative and administrative measures to ensure the special protection of the wild fauna species specified in Appendix II. The following will in particular be prohibited for these species:

a) all forms of deliberate capture and keeping and deliberate killing.

b) the deliberate damage to or destruction of breeding or resting sites.

c) the deliberate disturbance of wild fauna, particularly during the period of breeding, rearing and hibernation, insofar as disturbance would be significant in relation to the objectives of this Convention ...

Appendix II lists strictly protected fauna species, including 'Microchiroptera, all species except *Pipistrellus pipistrellus*'.

The 'Agreement on the Conservation of Populations of European Bats' (EUROBATS Agreement) was negotiated under the 'Convention for the Conservation of Migratory Wild Species' (Bonn Convention), and came into force in January 1994. The legal protection of bats and their habitats are given in Article III as fundamental obligations:

1. Each Party shall prohibit the deliberate capture, keeping or killing of bats except under permit from its competent authority.

2. Each Party shall identify those sites within its own area of jurisdiction which are important for the conservation status, including for the shelter and protection, of bats. It shall, taking into account as necessary economic and social considerations, protect such sites from damage or disturbance. In addition, each Party shall endeavour to identify and protect important feeding areas for bats from damage or disturbance.

The Agreement covers all European bat species.

OTHER MAMMAL PROTECTION

The Wildlife Act 1976; The Wildlife Amendment Act 2000. Some species are covered by the Habitats Directive (1992) (either Annex II or Annex IV, or lesser protection within Annex V). Some species are covered by the Bonn and Bern Conventions.

THE SUSTAINABLE DEVELOPMENT GOALS

Goal 15, Life on Land

Targets:

15.1   By 2020, ensure the conservation, restoration and sustainable use of terrestrial and inland freshwater ecosystems and their services, in particular forests, wetlands, mountains and drylands, in line with obligations under international agreements.

15.2   By 2020, promote the implementation of sustainable management of all types of forests, halt deforestation, restore degraded forests and substantially increase afforestation and reforestation globally.

15.3   By 2030, combat desertification, restore degraded land

and soil, including land affected by desertification, drought and floods, and strive to achieve a land degradation-neutral world.

15.4   By 2030, ensure the conservation of mountain ecosystems, including their biodiversity, in order to enhance their capacity to provide benefits that are essential for sustainable development.

15.5   Take urgent and significant action to reduce the degradation of natural habitats, halt the loss of biodiversity and, by 2020, protect and prevent the extinction of threatened species.

15.6   Promote fair and equitable sharing of the benefits arising from the utilization of genetic resources and promote appropriate access to such resources, as internationally agreed.

15.7   Take urgent action to end poaching and trafficking of protected species of flora and fauna and address both demand and supply of illegal wildlife products.

15.8   By 2020, introduce measures to prevent the introduction and significantly reduce the impact of invasive alien species on land and water ecosystems and control or eradicate the priority species.

15.9   By 2020, integrate ecosystem and biodiversity values into national and local planning, development processes, poverty reduction strategies and accounts.

15.A   Mobilize and significantly increase financial resources from all sources to conserve and sustainably use biodiversity and ecosystems.

15.B   Mobilize significant resources from all sources and at all levels to finance sustainable forest management and provide adequate incentives to developing countries to advance such management, including for conservation and reforestation.

15.C   Enhance global support for efforts to combat poaching and trafficking of protected species, including by increasing the capacity of local communities to pursue sustainable livelihood opportunities.

FAMILY QUIZ

1. What animal has the weirdest eating habits? Why?
2. If you had animal superpowers, what would you choose, and how would you use them?
3. Name three species of bat.
4. What animal has really flexible ribs?
5. How and where does a pine marten poo? Feel free to wriggle your hips to demonstrate.
6. If someone was to describe you as an animal, what animal would it be? Why?
7. If you could talk to the animals, which animal would you chat to, and what would you ask?
8. What colours can you see on a starling?
9. When making bird boxes, the entrance hole should suit the size of the bird. If you were to design your own hall door, what size and shape would you use to make it perfect for yourself?
10. How high can you squeak? (Usually smaller creatures can make higher-frequency sounds than bigger creatures, so I bet the kids will win this challenge.)
11. Some bats shout through their mouths, and others shout through their noses. Give a good yell of 'BAT!' and then try the same technique with your mouth closed, shouting through your nose. Which is louder? (You may need hankeys for this part of the quiz!)

12. Imagine you are a male blue tit, and are offering the female a range of houses to live in. What buildings would you choose?

13. What animal builds its own heating system? If you were to build your own heating system, how would it work?

14. Try doing an impression of a jackdaw scolding call. Make it as frightening as possible – remember that it has to scare intruders away.

YEAR PLANNER

Choose three things to do each month!

January

- Put out peanuts, dog food, scraps and fruit for badgers and foxes.
- Join the Irish Wildlife Trust.
- Fill the birdfeeders with a mix of seeds (sunflower hearts, Nyjer seeds, oil seed rape and peanuts) and fat balls.
- Plant some hedgerow and ivy against walls for goldfinches to nest in.
- Put up some bird boxes.
- Pledge your garden as a pollinator-friendly garden by signing up with the All-Ireland Pollinator Plan: *pollinators.ie/gardens*
- Join Butterfly Conservation Ireland.

February

- Put out peanuts, dog food, scraps and fruit for badgers and foxes.
- Fill the birdfeeders with a mix of seeds (sunflower hearts, Nyjer seeds, oil seed rape and peanuts) and fat balls.
- Put up a large kestrel or barn owl box.
- Clean out your kitchen presses and throw out the waste food for wildlife.
- Make a compost heap.

- Join the Irish Seed Savers and sign up to a course with them. You will learn some new skills and grow some unusual vegetables.
- Spring clean your garden shed and get rid of any pesticides, herbicides, poison and slug pellets (dispose of them carefully).

March

- Put out peanuts, dog food, scraps and fruit for badgers and foxes.
- Take part in the An Taisce National Spring Clean.
- Join the Irish Council Against Blood Sports.
- Put stickers on any large windows to prevent bird collisions.
- Take part in the National Bumblebee survey with the National Biodiversity Centre.
- Join The Organic Centre and sign up to a course with them: *theorganiccentre.ie*
- Plant a pollinator-friendly hanging basket.
- Buy yourself *The Irish Butterfly Book* by Jesmond Harding.

April

- Try some no-dig gardening.
- Take part in the An Taisce National Spring Clean, taking litter away before it can harm wildlife.
- Download a copy of the 'Water Pollution Indicator' from Inland Fisheries Ireland and try some kick sampling in your local stream to check its water quality: *fisheriesireland.ie*
- Join Bat Conservation Ireland.
- Try taking some plaster cast moulds of paw prints.
- Have a read of *Whittled Away* by Padraig Fogarty. His podcasts are fabulous too.

May

- Put all outdoor lights on a sensor timer. Make sure that lights aren't left on overnight.
- Slow down when driving. Most road kills of hares, rabbits, foxes and badgers take place in May, August and September.
- Have a no-mow May and let your grass grow.
- Join An Taisce.
- Learn traditional crafts in the annual weekend in the hills with the Centre for Environmental Education and Training (CELT): *celtnet.org*
- Take part in walks and talks in biodiversity week. Bring some children on a bat walk. They will never forget it.
- Plant some cabbages, turnips and garden nasturtiums just for the caterpillars of the small white butterfly.

June

- If you are lucky enough to have a bat roost in your house, join the midsummer bat count. Invite the neighbours around at dusk, open a few bottles of wine and count whatever comes out of your house. You can log the results with Bat Conservation Ireland.
- Take part in the backyard biodiversity survey with the National Biodiversity Data Centre. This involves checking your garden for 20 species of insect, amphibian and mammal, and logging whatever you find with them: *biodiversityireland. ie/surveys/backyard-biodiversity/*
- Buy a squirrel feeder and fill it.
- Join Coastwatch and take part in their marine litter surveys.

July

- Let the grass grow long. The shrews need it.
- Keep filling the squirrel feeder.
- Sign up to Green Foundation Ireland's mailing list. It's free of charge, and you will have access to many online talks and past events and will be invited to future events.
- If you can drive, sign up to Bat Conservation Ireland's car-based bat monitoring. They need people to drive transects and record bats on detectors to monitor bat populations.
- Make a garden pond.
- Join Birdwatch Ireland.

August

- Slow down when driving. Most road kills of hares, rabbits, foxes and badgers take place in May, August and September.
- Join Butterfly Conservation Ireland and take part in their walks.
- Take part in the Bat Conservation Ireland Daubenton's survey. This will involve walking along a waterway twice and noting numbers of Daubenton's bats at points along it. Full training is provided by Bat Conservation Ireland.
- Be really careful if you are using the garden strimmer. Watch out for hedgehogs.
- Take part in walks and talks during Heritage week.

September

- Buy some bat boxes and put them up.
- Slow down when driving. Most road kills of hares, rabbits, foxes and badgers take place in May, August and September.

- Treat yourself to a lovely ecological weekend away. Sign up to a course in Cloughjordan Eco Village: *thevillage.ie*
- Collect some horse chestnut conkers with the kids and make conker animals.
- Think about your heating system. Can you change from burning fossil fuels to using electric heating systems? Have a look at the grants available from SEAI.

October

- Be a voice for nature. Keep an eye out for repointing of stone bridges, churches and walls. Ask if they have been checked for bats.
- Make a woodpile and leave it for hibernating animals.
- Put out peanuts, scraps, dog food and fruit for badgers and foxes.
- Check bonfire piles for hedgehogs before Halloween.
- Fill the birdfeeders with a mix of seeds (sunflower hearts, Nyjer seeds, oil seed rape and peanuts) and fat balls.
- Treat yourself to some good wildlife books. Try Jesmond Harding's *The Irish Butterfly Book* if you didn't buy it already!
- Do a Halloween bat project with children. Use the resource from Bat Conservation Ireland: *learnaboutbats.com/bat-facts/our-irish-bats*
- Have a look at your pension. Is it an ethical one? Talk to your pension advisor about divesting from the fossil fuel industry.

November

- Plant a tree – ideally in open grassland in a field or a local community area. Talk to your local GP clinic or health centre about forest bathing and the health benefits of trees. See if they will allow you to plant one by their clinics.

- Cover any bare areas of soil with a crop such as mustard or comfrey.
- Put out peanuts, dog food, scraps and fruit for badgers and foxes.
- Build or buy a pine marten box and put it up.
- Fill the birdfeeders with a mix of seeds (sunflower hearts, Nyjer seeds, oil seed rape and peanuts) and fat balls.
- Sign up to the Birdwatch Ireland Garden Bird Survey. You can watch bird feeders all day and add to our scientific knowledge at the same time! *birdwatchireland.ie/our-work/surveys-research/research-surveys/irish-garden-bird-survey/*
- Plant bulbs for bees, such as crocus and snowdrops.

December
- Put out peanuts, dog food, scraps and fruit for badgers and foxes.
- Fill the birdfeeders with a mix of seeds (sunflower hearts, Nyjer seeds, oil seed rape and peanuts) and fat balls.
- Buy yourself a bat detector for Christmas.
- Take part in the Birdwatch Ireland Garden Bird Survey.
- Try to find a starling murmuration near you. You won't be disappointed.
- Plant some elder bushes and other fruit bushes, like redcurrants, blackcurrants and blackberries. You will share the fruit with the birds in summertime.

ANIMAL OF THE YEAR PLAN

Choose an animal you will dedicate the year to!

Animal Chosen:
Food:
   What food will it eat?
   When and how will you feed it?
   What can you plant to help it feed itself?

Water:
   Where will it drink? Do you need to provide a pond, birdbath or wet banks?

Home:
   Where will it live?
   Do you need to plant bushes or add nest boxes?

Thank you for taking time out for nature. Now for the fun bit – put this book into action and get started!